Oct 3, 2013

Nurturing Connection

Dear Sharon,

Thank you for all you do to nurture connection in families. Your work is brilliant and very much needed. Thank you for letting your light shine.

Love always,

Rebecca
Thompson

Nurturing Connection

What Parents Need to Know About Emotional Expression and Bonding

Rebecca Thompson, M.S.

The Consciously Parenting Project, LLC

Published in the United States by
The Consciously Parenting Project, LLC

Paperback Version
Original Source: Nurturing Connection: What Parents Need to Know About Emotional Expression and Bonding
May 2013 edition
ISBN: 978-0-9842756-9-4

Original Process: The Consciously Parenting Project, LLC
Created by: The Consciously Parenting Project, LLC

Illustrations by: Susan Graham
Book Design by: Lianne March

Special thanks to Shannon Livingston of Livingston Galleries for the cover photo. http://www.shannonlivingston.com

View My Website:
http://www.consciouslyparenting.com
http://www.holisticfamilyconsultant.com
http://iheartparenting.com
E-mail me: rebecca@consciouslyparenting.com

To all families who are struggling to find ways to connect and understand themselves and their children better.

With appreciation:

I am so very grateful for all the support I've had over the years it has taken me to write this book from many, many people. Without all the encouragement, support while scribbling on napkins, and listening to me talk endlessly about these ideas, this would simply not have been possible. I would need to write another book to thank everyone adequately, but I'll do my best in the space I have.

Special thanks to my precious boys, Zach and Josh, who have taught me so much about life and parenting. Thank you for being my teachers. I am eternally grateful.

To Lianne March, without whom The Consciously Parenting Project and this book would not have been possible. Thank you for seeing the vision and helping me to make all this a reality, for late night e-mails and brainstorms. You have my heartfelt thanks.

Amy Rost, the best book midwife ever. Thank you for your time, your attention, your passion, and going above and beyond the call of duty to help breathe life and clarity into this book.

With appreciation to Bethany Shetler, Wilma Vance, Sally Flintoff, MaryJo McHaney, Ammana Shaka, and Valerie Groves for your encouragement, your wisdom, and your passion for families who have adopted or fostered children. Your contributions to the earliest versions of this book were essential to its development.

To my friends who supported and encouraged me through the ups and downs of writing and life: Susan Graham, my cruising buddy, for your saint-like support and willingness to listen and wait, and to draw on napkins and other table coverings with me.

Debra Hart for living life on the other side of the worm hole, for reminding me to sing, for your honesty and clarity. Janet Conner for providing so much more than a space to write.

For professional inspiration that has deeply affected my work, thank you to Pam Leo, Ray Castellino, Mary Jackson, Lu Hanessian, Suzanne Arms, Lisa Reagan and Carrie Contey. Thank you for lighting the way for so many families around the world.

I am eternally grateful to all the families I've worked with over the years who have taught me so much about life, love, and the importance of remaining open and curious about ourselves and our loved ones. It isn't always the journey we thought we were going on, but it is the journey we were meant to make.

Rebecca Thompson, MS, MFT
Dunedin, FL
May, 2013

Contents

Introduction

Deepak Chopra spoke powerful words when he said,
"Love without action is meaningless and action without love
is irrelevant." I believe this speaks deeply to what nurturing
connected families is all about and what we all want when
we become parents. We need to realize that we convey our love,
or lack thereof, in everything we do with our children and our
partner. Nurturing connection is about finding ways to demonstrate love through our actions, as well as our way of being with
one another.

Nurturing our relationship with our children is the heart
and soul of consciously parenting. Nurturing relationships, once
they are established, is really an art. It is about remembering that
our children's need for connection is a primary factor in most of
their behavior. It is about recognizing that, in every parenting
situation, we have choices about how we respond to our children
and their behaviors. It is about seeing every parenting situation
as an opportunity to create connection or disconnection. It is
about looking at our everyday parenting situations and beginning
to see how we can choose connection. It is also about being able
to admit when something didn't go as planned, to forgive ourselves for not always being the parents we hope to be, and to
forgive our children for not always being the children we hope
they'd be.

When parenting situations challenge us, how we handle
them can create connection or disconnection in our relationship
with our children. We can imagine these situations as forks in
the road; there is one road sign, going off to the left, that says,
"Connection" and another, going off to the right, that says,
"Disconnection." At the fork, where the roads meet up, we have
choices, and the decisions we make can mean the difference
between peace and struggle, not only in that moment, but also in
the relationship as a whole. It is through these smaller, moment-

to-moment decisions that the stage is set and we and our children move closer together or further apart.

Most of our parenting information leads us further away from connection in the name of teaching our children what is right and wrong. In my own home growing up, I saw how parenting focused on behavior change alone led to more disconnection and the need for relationship repair. The advice given by "professionals" and implemented by my parents created a greater level of disconnection and chaos within my family. Parents need to teach their children appropriate behaviors, but they don't need to do so at the expense of the relationship.

Children who feel connected to you will want to please you—and they will. If they aren't acting in a way that is acceptable to you, there is something going on with them or something going on with you, and they're reacting to your energy or what is going on with your connection. The first of consciously parenting's eight guiding principles says, "All behavior is communication." When we are aware of what is going on beneath the surface, beneath the behavior—such as emotional regulation or dysregulation, unmet needs, or unresolved traumas—we can respond in a loving way rather than just reacting to the child's behavior. And responding lovingly nurtures the relationship. We need our children to have a strong relationship with us so that they can trust that we'll be there for them when they need us. And they really do need us. Behavior-focused parenting information uses pain, fear, punishment, isolation, shame, and coercion to manage our child's negative behavior. When we dole out punishments or focus on the behavior, our children learn that they cannot come to us. Instead, they seek out information and support from their peers—those with only a limited number of years on the planet and limited long-term decision-making skills. Relationship-focused parenting teaches our children to calm themselves down by reaching out to us when they're stressed. It teaches our children to come to us, the parents, to be supported through challenges and when they are having a hard time.

Whether we were parenting consciously from the beginning of our children's lives or we have worked hard to create more connection with our growing children, we need to understand that love and respect are co-created in a relationship. This idea can be challenging for us as parents, because most parenting information suggests that parenting is about the adult drawing the line in the sand and the child submitting. Many parents struggle with the expectation that their children just need to "do as I say when I say to do it." That method of parenting is about control. But control isn't co-creation; controlling your children isn't nurturing, nor is it realistic in a healthy relationship. This doesn't mean that your child doesn't have to do what you ask or that your own needs don't matter, especially as your children grow older. But when we stop and respect our children and their needs, as well as our own, we are modeling respectful, nurturing behaviors.

It is the day-to-day experiences we have as parents that determine whether our children learn appropriate behavior or not, whether our children learn to regulate their behavior and emotions or not, and whether we live in a peaceful environment where everyone respects everyone else's needs or not. It is our choice whether or not our children learn these things. If we are mindful of our parenting choices, we can create the family we want to have. Many times, we just are not aware that we have choices. Learning what those choices are is what this book is all about.

We'll look at common parenting situations with children of different ages and stages of development, and we'll discuss behavior-focused parenting strategies, which are what we normally see in our society, followed by a relationship-focused approach. The more that you are able to see examples of this paradigm shift, the more you will be able to apply it to your own parenting situations and circumstances.

Introduction

Please note that nurturing relationships doesn't mean that if we don't *always* make the best choice, we will have somehow failed as parents. We're going to have times where we end up creating disconnection because we're running on autopilot and parenting according to old road maps from our childhood. Nurturing relationships means that when we do make a mistake, we set it right and find ways to reconnect with our children, to prevent the need to totally repair the relationship. A pilot friend shared the example of how just a slight shift in the course set early in the flight can mean the difference between arriving at the destination and ending up in a different country. When we make small course shifts early in our parenting, it avoids the need for much larger or radical repair to our relationship later.

We'll also talk about how we can meet our children's connection needs and nurture the relationship when we are so busy. We always have places to go, things to do, email to check, TV to watch. We have laundry that never ends and dinners, lunches, and breakfasts that need to be planned and prepared. And many of us also hold down jobs outside the home. Since we clearly don't live in a simple world, we need to make our personal world simpler for the benefit of our families and our children— and ourselves. Even if we can't slow things down all the way, we can find ways to simplify and find ways to create a community of support around us.

Pam Leo points out in her book *Connection Parenting*, "We can either meet children's need for connection or we can spend our time dealing with the unmet need behaviors. Either way, we spend the time." When we can nurture our relationship with our children on a daily basis, going out of our way to create connection, everything is easier, and parenting is much more enjoyable.

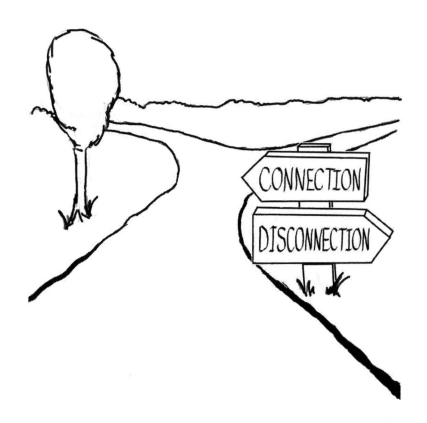

Chapter One

Choosing Nurturing Daily

At every level and every stage of development, there is either love—and with it, growth—or fear—and with it protection and a thwarting of growth.

Cell biologist Bruce Lipton

Chapter One

"Mom! You didn't get me my coconut water!" my nine-year-old son, Josh, yelled from the sofa.

"I'm really sorry, honey. I totally forgot."

Josh melted into tears, shouting his disappointment at me from the other room, imploring me to return to the store for the forgotten item—now!

This wasn't his norm. Normally if I forgot something from the store, he would be disappointed. He might ask me to get it when I go back to the store, but he wouldn't get demanding. He was clearly in distress. He was in survival mode, and his fight, flight, or freeze response had kicked in. Yes, over coconut water. Intellectually, I knew we just needed to stop. He was unable to think clearly or be rational. Now was not the time to explain to him why I couldn't go back to the store this minute or why he wasn't going to get what he wanted by yelling.

I was not far behind him, outside the comfortable realm of calm and connected. I was in my emotional brain, watching him melt down. I was tired. It had been an emotionally trying week for all of us, with lots of changes for everyone. Forgetting his coconut water was just the proverbial straw that broke the camel's back, the catalyst for the tears to flow and the stress to all come out.

I knew all this.

I asked myself if I had the capacity at that moment to really be with him, to just sit next to him and hear his feelings. I turned inward for a moment, amidst his shouts, to check in with myself. I acknowledged for myself that this had been a difficult few days. Clearly I needed to do something, though, as he was just getting louder.

I checked in with myself again. What did I need right now? I took a deep breath. I set aside the sweet potatoes I was preparing for dinner and the voices in my head saying that he shouldn't be so upset over coconut water. I looked over at my son, and I tried to put myself in his shoes.

Everything in his world had been changing. What did he need?

He didn't actually *need* coconut water. He needed comfort, predictability, for something to be familiar. He needed me to see him, feel him, and be with him.

What Do Our Children *Really* Need?

More than anything, our children need connection with us. And we need to feel connected to them.

Research has shown that incorporating the following six things into your daily parenting activities creates more opportunities for connection and nurturing to happen:

- Physical touch
- Emotional presence
- Simplicity
- Rhythm and rituals
- Community
- Play

To avoid feeling overwhelmed, we may choose to focus on only one area at a time and see what feels best to us and to our children. Each nurturing choice we make helps everyone in the family to feel more connected.

Physical Touch

We all need touch every day. Touch is the first sense our babies develop when they are growing during pregnancy, and gentle touch is one of the most important ways to bond with our babies and young children. As babies, we receive much of our information about the world through our skin and how we are touched. We naturally touch our children when we change their diapers or clothes and hopefully when we are feeding them. This amount of physical touch will ensure our children's survival, but in order to thrive, they need the felt security created by the physical touch of those they love. Being aware of how important touch is can make a huge difference in our connection with our children.

At the beginning of 2012, I took a certification class for infant massage, from Infant Massage USA and teacher Linda Storm. As part of the class, we taught parents how to use gentle massage techniques to connect with their babies and nurture their relationship. I was amazed at how much more some of the parent-baby pairs were able to connect when the parents just gently touched their babies and watched their baby's responses.

In the class, I learned that massage—and gentle touch of any kind—supports the bonding and attachment process regardless of what has happened in the relationship up to that point. If you have a connected relationship with your baby or child, adding physical touch will deepen that connection. If you have a strained relationship or a difficult beginning, adding in gentle physical touch will support your child and your bond with him or her.

On a physical level, gentle physical touch releases oxytocin, also known as "the cuddle hormone," in both the baby and the parent, creating a deeper connection between them. Massaging your baby or young child also decreases your stress hormones and increases your own relaxation. For nursing moms, massaging the baby increases prolactin levels, which are associated with a good milk supply. If your baby or young child is experiencing gas, colic, physical or psychological tension, or disorganization of the nervous system (the symptoms of which include startling easily, extra sensitivity, frequent crying, and difficulty being soothed, and the causes of which might be a difficult birth or a stay in neonatal intensive care, or NICU), massage can provide relief. And when the baby feels better, the parents feel better.

The most important part of any kind of nurturing touch is that it is responsive to your baby's or child's cues. Recently,

I was entranced by a video of a midwife giving a newborn a bath. It was not much like the baths I used to give my newborns. There was such gentleness in each and every touch. The midwife moved very slowly, responding to the baby, and the baby was clearly relaxing in her hands. I felt myself relaxing just watching the video!

Each and every time we touch our babies and young children—even for the most mundane reasons—is an opportunity to nurture our relationship by bringing in the element of loving touch. So consider how you approach your daily parenting tasks and ask yourself what you could do to increase the loving touch in each of those activities, from dressing your young children to helping them brush their teeth, from getting a child into a car seat to leaving the house to run an errand. Other ways to stay in touch with your baby might include carrying her in a sling throughout the day, making time for snuggles, or giving lots of hugs as your children grow older.

Nurturing physical touch is also important for our older children, and for us as adults. Our bigger kids benefit from hugs, back rubs, and foot massages just as much as our younger kids, and need it just as much, if not more. I encourage my adult clients to seek out gentle physical touch for themselves in their own lives, whether it is making sure they receive lots of hugs from family and friends or making an appointment for a massage or other bodywork technique (such as cranial-sacral therapy, Jin Shin Jyutsu, Jin Shin Tara, Reiki, and Masgutova Method, just to name a few). Our older kids can benefit from each of those modalities as well, if they are available to us. When we have had our own physical-touch needs met, it is easier for us to meet the physical-touch needs of our children.

When I walked over to the couch and sat down next to Josh, I asked him what he needed. He shrugged his shoulders. I asked if he wanted a hug, and he said yes. I gave him a big hug and held him gently for a minute or so. I talked to him softly. After I finished giving him his hug, he lifted his feet into the air and placed them in my hands. He wanted some nurturing touch. This is something that we do on a regular basis, and I really love that he was able to ask for it once he had calmed down just a bit.

> You need four hugs per day for survival, eight per day for maintenance, and twelve per day for growth.
>
> Virginia Satir

Emotional Presence

What do children need from us after their basic needs (food, clothing, shelter) are met? They need our emotional presence. They need someone to give them their complete and undivided attention. They need someone whose eyes light up when they walk (or crawl) into the room.

When I was babysitting in high school, I often thought that parents were really detached from their kids. I would walk into a room (fresh, well rested, with a new set of eyes and ears) and would listen fully and completely to the children. I would see them relax, and they would often go off to play on their own. Parents, by contrast, were often short with their children. They appeared distracted and didn't stop what they were doing to be with their children. As a nonparent, I couldn't really understand this behavior. I knew these parents loved their children more than anything else in the world, so why would they treat their children like they didn't care about them? (When I became a parent myself, I understood. These parents were exhausted, and they had called me to come watch their children so they could take time off and recharge. They were the smart ones!)

What I was observing was a lack of something we now refer to as *emotional presence*. Being fully with another person means that you aren't multitasking (paying the bills, texting a friend, watching television, or thinking about what you need to do or say after the person in front of you finishes whatever it is that they're saying). Your mind is focused on the person in front of you, and your actions show you are listening to that person. When you're a parent, it means that you aren't focused on doing something with or for your child (solving the problem, getting your child's teeth brushed, or getting your child upstairs for bed), but you are focused on simply being.

When we can simply be with our children, we might just notice that they are trying to tell us something. Maybe they're saying they need us to connect with them in a playful way before we head upstairs for bed. Maybe they need us to hold them for a few minutes, or they want to finish what they're doing before we impose our agenda on them. Being emotionally present allows us to see the things that we might have otherwise missed. It doesn't mean that what we want our children to do at a particular time isn't important; it means that we respect them enough to take time to notice their needs as well as our own.

Here are some tips for cultivating your ability to be emotionally present with your children:

1. Recognize when what your child is doing is different from what you thought would happen.

2. Stop. Quiet your mind. Set aside your own agenda for the moment, and ask what your child is communicating to you through his behavior.

3. Ask yourself how you can connect with your child. (Hint, get down on her level and look her in the eyes. Connect with your own inner guidance. See the world through her eyes.)

4. Put aside everything else other than the relationship with the amazing being before you. When you do this, your child is much more likely to be able to be cooperative.

5. Remember that every challenge with your child is an opportunity to learn more about yourself and your child. It is an opportunity to learn to connect with your child in a deeper way.

How do you feel about the idea of setting aside time to just be emotionally present with your children? If you feel like it is just another to-do item to mark off your list at the end of the day, your children aren't going to benefit in the same way they will if you're happy to do it. If your partner or a friend agreed to spend time with you, but didn't actually want to spend time together, how would you feel? If you find that you're feeling overwhelmed or underwhelmed at the thought of devoting time to just being with your child, find the place within you that is curious about who this little one showing up today really is. What matters to him? Who does she look like when she smiles?

While I was rubbing Josh's feet, I stayed relatively quiet. I was watching him and allowing myself to just be with him. I put myself in his shoes. I put dinner on hold.

I wasn't there with him long before I felt his whole body relax. I let him know I saw how many things had been changing in his life right then and how it seemed like he just needed something to be the same right now. He nodded and snuggled back into my arms. This is what happens when parents put their own agendas aside and are simply emotionally present with their children.

Simplicity

Children today lead busy lives. Between playgroups, daycare, school, homework, music lessons, athletics, watching television, eating, and sleeping, our children have schedules that would make most of us feel exhausted just reading about them. But all of these things are essential for a healthy childhood, aren't they? Not necessarily.

When I was a child, we didn't have as much technology in our lives as we do today. I recently was talking to my children about what life was like when I was young, and I found myself saying things like, "We only had three television channels. Cartoons were only on Saturday morning and ended at 11 a.m. We got an answering machine when I was in high school. The first computer I used was for my high school term paper, and it couldn't get online."

So what did I do with myself if I wasn't texting, watching three hundred television channels, and using a computer? I spent a lot of time outside, climbing trees, trying to catch tadpoles in one of the neighborhood ponds, and laying in the grass to watch the clouds race by on the wind. When I was older, I did take some music lessons and acting and dance classes. I participated in community theater. I sang with the jazz band, with the show choir, and in musicals. But the basic rhythm to my day was a slow one. It wasn't until I was in high school that every second of my day seemed to be filled, with sleeping, eating, school, homework, and practices.

Today, elementary-school children experience this young-adult level of stress and lack free time to just be. We don't rate time for just being very highly on our list of necessities in our society in general. Children need time to play with no one giving directions. Children need time when their parents are just sitting and playing with them—with no agenda and no rush to hurry up and get on to something more important. Organizations like the Alliance for Childhood, an organization focusing on research for optimal child development and pioneering a movement to bring play back into the kindergarten, are now necessary to help us to understand what it is that our children are missing by having schedules that are too full and academics that start too early.

How can we help our children? Here are some tips:

- For very young children, limit their activities outside the home.

- Limit media exposure and time on computer, television, cell phone, and other electronic devices whenever possible—both for your children and yourself. You'll find you have more time to accomplish tasks. Create a set time for computer or television after your children are sleeping.

- Make a list of the most important things you need to spend your time doing. Release those things that you don't need to do now. But make sure there is at least one activity on the list that you really enjoy doing. Don't simplify away your fun!

- Create a community of support to share the tasks that everyone needs to do.

- If you work from home, clearly define work time and family time. Turn off the cell phone when you're having family time. If necessary, let your clients and/or coworkers know when family time is.

- Choose one task that you'd like to find a way to make easier—say, dinner preparation—and work on creating simplicity around that task. In the case of dinner, you might purchase meals from a place like Dinner Done; create a food-making co-op with some friends, who share the tasks of buying ingredients and preparing meals; make very simple meals with few ingredients;

or find an online meal planner complete with selected
sale ingredients from your local stores.

- Consider voluntary pre-kindergarten (VPK) and kindergarten experiences carefully. Young children do not need
early academics. The countries that do the best academi-
cally don't begin formal instruction of children until
age seven. Instead of sending your children to school,
create playgroups where they can be with other children
and where you can be with other parents. Consider
homeschooling or educational settings where children
are allowed to be children, particularly when they are
young, such as Waldorf, Montessori, Reggio Emilia,
Sudbury, or others schools that may be part of local
educational movements.

When everything is changing in a child's life, simplicity becomes
even more important. The rest of the evening, Josh and I slowed
down, pulled out his favorite toys (Legos), and snuggled together
while he went to sleep. I did my best to create an environment
where everything slowed down for both of us. We didn't need
to go to the store or have a play date with a friend. He needed
the time to just be home and settle.

Rhythm and Rituals

When our children are young, they need to feel that their lives
are predictable to some extent. Creating a sense of rhythm in
our lives helps nurture our children. We can create some times
to connect with our children in predictable ways, particularly
around the transitions during our days. For example, some
families have a song they sing in the morning to wake everyone
up. Other families have a time of prayer or a verse that they
speak together after they read a story at night.

Chapter One

As an attachment parent, I found myself saying that my family didn't need to create a rhythm, since our rhythm was that I was always there with my son, and I met his needs as I saw them come up. But as my children have grown older, I have seen the wisdom of creating a general rhythm to the day (a quiet activity followed by a more active time followed by a quieter time) and how much that rhythm helps everyone to learn to regulate their emotional state and behavior.

A rhythm is different from a schedule because it is flexible and allows for the changing needs of the entire family. Instead of maintaining a rigid bedtime at 7:30 PM and naptime at 1:30, we know that we are aiming to have bedtime and naptime at those times. Creating a rhythm is about mindfully guiding our children into and out of states of calm and states of activity.

Rhythm can be created through rituals. These rituals can be quite simple, especially with young children. In our family, one of our little rituals is that, each night, I go in and sit on my older son's bed for about fifteen minutes. We sit and talk about the day or whatever else he'd like to bring up. I'm there with him, and he has my attention for that little while. And he can count on it. With my younger son, our bedtime ritual consists of sharing what happened during our day, followed by lighting a candle and saying a verse we wrote together. ("Good night, sun. Good night, stars. Good night, Mom and Dad. Good night, Zach [his brother], and good night to me. Thank you for this beautiful day!")

The best daily rituals are those that involve you being completely emotionally present with your child. I strongly suggest spending time together in the morning, before the day even gets started. When my older son was returning to public school after several years of homeschooling, he was getting up early and leaving with his father as he went into work. I didn't have to get up, but I did, because I knew that connecting with my son was important as he made his transition from home to school each day. We would spend time just sitting close together on the couch in the low light of early morning. We usually didn't do much talking. I would just sit and be with him, taking in where he was and focusing on remaining present with him. I wasn't trying to fix him or get him to tell me something, and I know that he appreciated the effort it took for me to get out of bed when I didn't have to do it.

You might also consider adding in a special ritual for you and your children as a part of your weekly rhythm. One dad always went out with his daughter to get bagels on Sunday mornings before church. This bagel run became a special time for them to spend together. Another family had a Saturday-morning ritual of making chocolate chip–banana pancakes together and sitting down to eat them as a family.

Once we arrived at bedtime, I was sure it was comforting for Josh to begin his nighttime routine. Right now, our bedtime routine is simple: put on pajamas, brush teeth, read a chapter in a book or tell a story about our day, and then snuggle off to sleep. With so many things changing, he and I told the story of everything that was going on in his life. Telling that story didn't mean complaining about the situation, but simply acknowledging everything that was going on for him—especially all the changes. He was excited that his grandparents would be visiting, but with those visits come lots of different schedules. He was very excited about visiting the boat with them during his spring break, but we acknowledged how his going alone with them to the boat would be different than having me with them when they went. When his experiences were unpacked and acknowledged, he was able to drift off to sleep.

Community

When our children are small, we need to be together. But the idea that we must raise our children in relative isolation with only one or two people meeting most of their needs is a relatively new phenomenon.

When I began my parenting journey, I felt a great need to have other parents around me who were raising their children in a similar way. I went to great lengths to cultivate that for myself without realizing how important it also was for my son to be in community.

One of the most profound moments happened when my oldest son was only a couple months old. He was fussy and colicky and had been crying for most of the day. And so had I. My husband was working late, and I didn't expect relief of any kind for another several hours. We lived in a townhouse, and the walls were certainly not impervious to the sounds of a baby crying. When my neighbor came home from her teaching job in the midafternoon, she heard the crying and came over. The front door wasn't locked, so she let herself in and came back to the room where I was holding Zach. Without a word, she leaned over and gently took the crying baby from my arms. At this point, I started crying more. It was unexpected and much needed relief.

No matter how amazing you are as a parent, no matter how much you intend to be there for your baby or young child every second of every day, no one can do it all—no one. And our children benefit from other loving, "fresh" caregivers who can be with them on a regular basis.

The most important people to include in your child's community are relatives. Grandparents, aunts, uncles, cousins, and other extended family members necessarily have a little vested interest (most of the time) in making sure that your child is loved and cared for. When possible, encourage extended family to participate with your child in whatever way they are able.

As our children become more aware of the world around them, it is important for them to have the experience of being cared for by other loving adults. When the child feels that the world is safe and he will be cared for no matter who is nearby, it helps him understand that the world is safe. Our children need the experiences that can be provided by someone who isn't thoroughly exhausted. Just follow your own instincts about who is safe to leave your child with and who you might want to be nearby, until you feel more comfortable extending the distance away from your child. Respect your own pace.

Encouraging Long-Distance Family Relationships

Many extended families live far apart and don't have the luxury of being together on a regular basis. This makes it more challenging for parents who lack in-person support and more difficult for extended family to cultivate relationships with little ones. But you can find creative ways for your child and extended family to stay in touch between visits, which should also be planned as often as is practical, because there is no substitute for being in the same room with loved ones.

My mother, who lives in Indiana, began telling stories with my oldest son, Zach, when we moved away to Florida. They would spend hours on the phone, having adventures with characters they had invented, and it really helped them to connect with each other. They both looked forward to their regular phone calls and to seeing what would happen next in their story.

(continued)

With the advent of Skype and other video chats,
I hear that many families use this technology to
connect with each other when they are far apart.
It requires a bit of creativity at first, but is well
worth the effort to find out what works best for
your child.

When extended family does come to town,
allow for transition time. Avoid handing your
young child off to the grandparents when they
walk in the door so you can go out on a date,
for example. Allow a day or two (or more,
depending upon your child's age and
temperament), and watch for signs that
your child is ready to be with just them.

The more early trauma that we, as parents, have experienced, the more likely we will become overwhelmed when trying to care for our children by ourselves. It is important to recognize when we are overwhelmed and to create a community of support, so that someone can be connecting with our child when we are taking that much needed break.

As children grow older, they need to have time with other children. Children have historically grown up with lots of other children around, and that peer-to-peer companionship is an essential part of growing up. Most children today spend most of their time on electronics or in structured activities. Children need time to be with other children, building, creating, and imagining. This is where they learn how to work together and to work out their differences, with our support when needed. These are much-needed skills in our world today; most adults don't lose their jobs because they aren't skilled, but because they lack the social skills to work well with others. Our children need the opportunities to refine those skills in childhood, when the stakes aren't quite so high. When all their time is structured or they are plugged into electronics, they aren't interacting with others, and they aren't learning critical social skills. When they are engaging with another child (or two) to build a fort or have an adventure camping in the backyard, they are developing those important social skills. This time with others can be monitored more closely until you feel confident that either your child can handle difficulties or that your child will come to you if needed.

Some of the best experiences my children and I have had have been when we have gathered with other families for a task, such as food preparation. While the parents work together, the children play together nearby, free to come and go from the food prep and be with the children as desired. No one parent becomes exhausted, and the children are generally occupied. This type of group activity works great if you can find like-minded parents who can work together well to handle any challenges. Truly, it is worth the effort!

You may notice that in my story about Josh, he and I were alone, as many of us parents often are, for various reasons. It is rare when someone is readily available to come and provide additional help when we need it. While Josh's grandparents happened to be staying nearby, they were otherwise occupied for the evening. Had I been more overwhelmed, I would have reached out to a friend or other family member and asked them to just be with me and support me while I supported Josh.

In this situation, I felt that Josh really did need to be with just me, and so I probably wouldn't have had someone else come in to play with him so that I could have a break. However, there are situations when that's just what I've done. You know what you and your family need more than anyone else. Trust that you will know what is needed for any given situation.

A Word about Community for Parents

We nurture our relationships with our children when we are feeling nurtured and supported ourselves. When we have a group of people who are looking out for us and for our children, it makes us all stronger, happier, and more present. We weren't meant to raise our children in our own houses alone, by ourselves. We need others to support us, and we need to support others. The challenge is that most of us have never experienced this type of community before, nor do we know how to start to create it.

So what's a parent to do? Perhaps start by having a conversation with other parents. You might be surprised to hear that you are really not alone! If you have a local parenting-support group, such as one through Attachment Parenting International, La Leche League, or your birthing center, hospital, school, or homeschooling group, that would be a good place to start. You can also look on the "Finding Your Tribe" section of the *Mothering.com* community forums or post your location and your circumstances. (That's how I found Lianne March, a dear friend and the mother who has worked with me to make the Consciously Parenting Project possible.)

For many years, I've had a vision of women sitting around a fire in a large circle, talking while they take care of the tasks that need to be done for their tribe. Even though this type of circle isn't the literal reality of my day-to-day life, I pay attention to what circumstances I can change in my life to give myself the type of companionship I've envisioned. Because I've moved frequently, I've often found myself knowing no one in my local community. To connect with others, I began by searching for an online community. I found other parents on similar journeys, and connecting with them helped me see what was possible for me to find or create. As I became more aware of what I was looking for, I consciously created community for myself in my daily life. For a while, I was part of a group that worked together to plan meals, share the food-buying process, and prepare food.

We weren't always together, but having the support of others who were able to make meals lifted a large part of the burden of that aspect of parenting, which I felt overwhelmed by when my children were young and my husband was working long hours and days away from home.

Remember that there are nonparents out there who have more time, energy, and resources than parents who are in the trenches. When you're looking for support around you, consider those who may not have children. These people may enjoy spending time with your children, either when you're home or out running errands. Adult relatives and adult friends, as well as teens, can be a great help. One of the best resources I found was a local homeschooling group that included several children who enjoyed playing with younger children. I met a preteen boy who I paid to come over and play with my children while I was home. He had a great time with my kids, my boys adored him, and I was able to count on getting some extra work done or having a few hours to myself.

The most important thing to realize is that if you aren't looking for community, you aren't going to find it. Start by opening your eyes to see what might be right in front of you.

Play

We take parenting really seriously. Sometimes, we take it way too seriously. We've joined the adult world, with all of its adult responsibilities, and taken on the duties of running a household with children. Someone needs to take out the trash and remember to buy the trash bags. We have to be somewhere at a certain time of the day, so we need to get everyone ready to go and out the door so we'll be on time. Life gets reduced to schedules, commitments, and things we need to do. Life becomes only about survival.

But survival isn't nurturing. While our basic survival needs must be met for us to be able to access our ability to play, survival alone isn't enough to create a healthy family. In other words, if we're struggling because we don't have enough to eat, or we aren't physically or emotionally safe, we can't move into a place of play. But when we're safe, when our basic needs are met, we can play. And when we realize that, in terms of having a thriving family, getting to play is just as important as getting a good meal and enough sleep, we can make a conscious effort to add more play into our lives.

As I wrote about in my first book, *Consciously Parenting: What it Really Takes to Raise Emotionally Healthy Families,* there were several years after the death of my newborn when everyone in our family was overwhelmed and in survival mode. One of the best signs that my family was coming out of survival mode was when my eight-year-old son laughed. I hadn't realized that he hadn't laughed in a long time until his giggles reverberated across the room and caught my attention. Indeed, nothing had been funny for a long time.

Take a play inventory. What does play look like for your children? Are they active or passive when they play? What activities are they drawn to? Do they like a good word puzzle or a game of tag? Do they have time for independent play, as well as time to play with you or play with friends?

And what's the last playful thing you did with your child? When I think about the last few days with my kids, I can list the birthday parties we attended and all the fun they had, but I have to think a little harder about when we actually played together and what that playtime looked like for us. When our children are very young, we often spend time playing with them, either for fun or to help them engage and learn from the world around them. As our children grow older, they become more distracted by outside influences and activities, but it is still important for us to create time to play with our children.

In 2011, I interviewed Howard Moody, a play expert, and watched him play with my kids in order to demonstrate how to facilitate play with children. It was so much fun! What struck me the most was how little I was actually getting onto the floor to play with my kids and how much they loved it when I did. I was able to watch my children's excitement as Howard played with them. Then I joined in and watched as they became even more engaged. I hadn't heard my kids laugh so hard for a long time, and I was inspired to see what I could do to add more play into our lives.

Before Josh went to bed on his difficult evening, he and I got down on the floor and played Legos together. Play is how children unwind. Had it not been so cold and dark that night, I probably would have considered taking him to swim or to play outside, so he could release more energy. But I could also see that he had experienced a good release when he cried and expressed himself. He needed some quiet playtime. We played together for a little while, and then when I felt he was ready, I moved into the next room to finish making our dinner, and he continued to play alone. This playtime was very regulating for him. Had he needed me to stay with him, I probably would have scrapped my dinner plans and ordered a pizza.

Schedule Playtime Daily

So many children have every moment of their days planned. If your children are in school, chances are that they are getting very little unstructured time—time when nothing is planned for them. Children need unstructured time to imagine, create, explore, invent, and be in the quiet to connect with themselves. (We, as adults, need this time, too.) Even if our children are not in school, most of us tend to fill up our days with structured activities, and even though those activities may seem fun, the time we spend doing them is still structured.

The biggest obstacle to playtime is often that we, as parents, don't prioritize it. We don't recognize its importance. Sometimes unstructured playtime means that we're present with our children during their playtime, even if we're doing something else in the same room with them. One of the ideas I took from Waldorf education is to knit or do some other quiet handwork while the children play. When I'm knitting, a calm comes over me—and my child who is playing in that space.

If you feel like getting down on the floor with your child, I encourage you to allow your child to take the lead with playtime. See what your child likes, imagines, explores, and join her in this play, rather than adding in your own agenda about how you think play should be happening.

As children grow older, having time to play with other children becomes more important. While some playtime may have a structure, such as when children are playing video games, I encourage unstructured playtime with friends, as well. A pile of sheets and blankets, along with some clothespins, can go a long way when two kids work together.

With all the distractions, sometimes our kids need a little help getting started to play on their own, but it is important for development that they have these opportunities daily.

Our children need not only time to play every day, but also time to play *with us* every day. As discussed earlier in this chapter, whether our children are babies or toddlers or teenagers, they need time—perhaps five to twenty minutes—every day when we aren't washing dishes, planning a meal, trying to rush everyone out the door, or telling them what to do, but instead are fully present with them and doing something they want to do. It is critically important that every day you set aside time when you can just be with your children in the moment. What do they want to tell you? Show you? Do with you? Do they want to play outside or inside? Do they want to be active or quiet?

Parents often ask when this special playtime together needs to happen. This timing is as individual as each family. Some families have special time in the morning before work. Other families find that afternoon works well. With my children, the time after dinner seems to work well, because we're all well fed and settled from our day. Sometimes we go down to our community's private clubhouse and play one of the games there—table tennis or pool—at the kids' request. Other times, I plop down on the floor with Josh, and join him as he builds his latest Lego creation.

In addition, my husband and I often make up stories to tell our boys as a part of our special time together each night. My youngest son, now age nine, and I co-create ongoing sagas about a crazy group of hamsters (10,000 of them, to be exact). These hamsters now live on Hamster Island, which is a tiny island, just big enough for an airport, in the Gulf of Mexico. They solve mysteries and have many other traveling adventures, from cruising to jumping off the "Hampire" State Building in New York City. The most important part is that we both look forward to our fun time together and the adventures the hamsters will have next.

Every day looks a little bit different, and life in general certainly looks different, now that my boys are nine and fourteen, than it did when they were much younger. Each family's playtime is going to look different. The key is to be open to what your child shows an interest in and have a willingness to enter into your child's world.

Unstructured Playtime: A Space for Feelings

When you start to create unstructured time and space for children who haven't had it before, you may notice that they're unsure what to do with themselves. You may also see behaviors that you're not sure what to do with. When we ourselves slow down and take a break from our busy lives, we may notice that our feelings are much closer to the surface. The same thing happens to our children. We all, adults and children alike, need space to allow our feelings to bubble up. When we start to create the space for our children to have more free, explorative play, it is best for us to be nearby to support them if feelings begin to surface.

If our children have parts of their story, or background, they haven't yet integrated, those parts may come up in their unstructured play. Integration is a concept that was introduced to me by parenting experts Ray Castellino and Mary Jackson in *Little People, Big Challenges,* a series of audio interviews they did for the Consciously Parenting Project. When something overwhelming happens to a child (or adult), the experience often happens too quickly for us to process everything about it. With young children who don't have the words to talk about what they're experiencing, their story will show up in their behaviors and in the way they struggle with certain events in their life. Integration is the process of slowing down and connecting with your child, so that he or she can fully process all the emotions of an overwhelming experience in connection with you. Both integration and its sister concept, story sharing, are described in detail in the "Story Sharing" audio program from the *Little People, Big Challenges* series. Castellino and Jackson discuss children's stories and offer guidelines for supporting your children as they share and integrate their stories. These guidelines may be helpful if you notice something coming up for your child during his or her unstructured play.

Bethany's parents were making an effort to give their four-year-old daughter unstructured playtime each day, and they wanted her to spend time on her own in her room for ten or fifteen minutes each morning. Bethany often protested going into her room by herself, but after a little while, she would usually play just fine on her own. One day after playtime, her parents discovered that she had pulled all the stuffing out of one of her stuffed animals. They talked to Bethany about her stuffed animal and how it needed to be treated, and they helped her to put it back together. The next day, the stuffing was again removed. Clearly, Bethany was communicating something, but what?

For Bethany, being separated from her parents for solo playtime was too much for her to handle. Perhaps ten to fifteen minutes was too long. Maybe something was coming up when she was alone. Her story included being placed for adoption and spending time in complete isolation in a NICU, with no one visiting her, before she came home with her adoptive parents. These parts of her story might have been the reason that being separated from her parents during playtime was distressing. She may have needed some support in order to integrate these parts of her story. Then she would be able to conquer the developmental milestone of spending time on her own.

Principle 3 of consciously parenting states, "A need met will go away; a need unmet is here to stay."[1] Bethany's parents wanted her to be able to play by herself, but Bethany wasn't ready to handle that unstructured playtime on her own. With time, patience, and some space, Bethany was able show her parents her story. Using Castellino and Jackson's story-sharing guidelines, her parents were able to help her integrate her experience of being little and alone in the hospital. Then Bethany was able to play on her own and not need to have a parent physically present with her during her unstructured playtime.

If, like Bethany's parents, you notice that your child is trying to tell you something with his behavior, observe what is happening. What feelings are you seeing? What feelings come up for you while you watch? Does your child do the same thing over and over again? Sometimes a previous event in your child's life may come to mind as you're watching. When this happens, it means that the event you're remembering is probably important. Telling your child the story of that event it is often a key part of your child's process of integrating it (and many times, also for your own integration process).

---

[1] See Consciously Parenting: What It Really Takes to Raise Emotionally Healthy Families, Book I of the Consciously Parenting Series, for all eight principles.

Play: Not Just for Kids

According to the *Oxford Dictionaries* online, play is when we "engage in activity for enjoyment and recreation rather than a serious or practical purpose." Kids are all about play. It is the way they learn about their world. Playing with our children can not only remind us adults that not everything has to be serious or practical, but can also soothe the rough spots like a balm and add more connective glue between us and our children. It's magic.

There are lots of ways to play with your children, and the best ideas come from just watching them. But to get you started, here are a few playful things you can do with your children:

- Skip instead of walking.

- Sing a silly song.

- Dance your way to dinner.

- Pretend you are a train and let your kids "climb aboard" onto your back as you move to the "station."

- Play wrestle.

- Tell stories.

- Use puppets or finger puppets.

- Play peek-a-boo, even when your kids are a little older.

(continued)

Playtime isn't just for kids. It is actually vitally important that we, as adults, find fun ways to play. Playing gets us out of our beta brainwave state—a go, go, go, do, do, do state that takes us out of connection with others—and into alpha, a more relaxed brainwave state. And when we can relax a bit more into our own versions of play, we have more emotional space for our children.

So what can you do to add more playful fun to your adult life? Climb a tree, paint a picture, fly a kite, color pictures in a coloring book, sing a song, learn to play an instrument, skip down a street, or have a pillow fight with a friend. Or come up with your own ideas. No matter what you do, adding more play to your days will benefit you and everyone around you, including your children.

Play at the Fork in the Road

Play is usually the last thing most of us think about when we have an emotionally dysregulated child. Most of us go into logical, fix-it mode or become really task oriented. For example, if you're trying to get your child into the car and your child is refusing to get in (a good sign that he needs help regulating), you are probably going to think of strategies for talking your child to getting into the car, rationalizing with your child about why he needs to get into the car *now,* and perhaps even adding your own dysregulation to the mix. We all do it, especially when we're stressed out or in a hurry.

But what if, when you're at this fork in the road, you wanted to take the opportunity to connect with your child instead of creating more disconnection? One way to do that is through play. Play is a wonderful way to connect with your child and to regulate everyone's emotions. It can be especially helpful during transition times, such as when our child is getting out of bed in the morning, moving to the table to eat, having a diaper changed, leaving the house, getting into the stroller, going to school, taking a bath, or going to bed at night.

Marley was just two years old, and her mother, Karla, had basically decided that they just weren't going to go anywhere in the car anymore. Every time she tried to get Marley into the car, the stress was over the top, and Karla was at the end of her rope. Their Toyota had become an unintentional battlefield, and going anywhere just didn't seem worth the stress. Luckily, they lived in a town small enough that they could walk everywhere, but Karla knew avoiding the car wasn't a permanent solution.

I could feel Karla's tension as she talked to me about her car experiences. I suggested that maybe some play that involved getting into the car without actually going anywhere could help Marley to start to become friends with the Toyota. Karla decided to give it a try. She and Marley would go and sit in the car to have playtime. They'd sit together in the Toyota, singing songs, playing with finger puppets, reading stories. Within a week, Marley was asking to play in the car.

A few days later, Karla was feeling brave and decided to put Marley into her car seat to sing a song. To Karla's surprise and delight, Marley let her mom not only put her in the car seat, but buckle her as well! Not wanting to push it too much, Karla went up to the front seat and drove around the block, continuing to sing to Marley as they went. When they got back home, Karla was excited and delighted. They had shifted the pattern! Now, at four years old, Marley loves the car, and her view had changed because of play.

When we can remember to add play to a situation in which our child is emotionally dysregulated, we can not only help them regulate, but also potentially change an unhelpful pattern and create connection, instead of more disconnection, with our children.[2]

Now that we've explored some of the strategies for nurturing our relationships with our children, we'll be taking a more in-depth look at where we might get stuck and what we can do about it.

Questions to Ponder

- Identify your own forks in the road. What situations do you find yourself repeatedly in with your children? What would you like to try the next time it happens? Choose one strategy from this chapter that you'd like to implement and begin to envision yourself doing this new behavior *before* you face the challenging situation with your child. You actually begin to change your brain just by visualizing what you'd like to do. Give it a try!

- How frequently do you spend time with your children in which you are giving them the gift of loving touch? When we're disconnected from our children, loving touch tends to decrease. (And as the mother of a fourteen-year-old, I can tell you that it decreases naturally as our children grow older.) What can you do to increase loving touch with your children?

---

[2] For more information about regulation and dysregulation, please check out *Consciously Parenting: What It Really Takes to Raise Emotionally Healthy Families,* Book I of the Consciously Parenting Series.

- Are there areas of your life or your children's lives that need simplifying? Are you too busy? Choose something that you can let go of and replace it with some quiet time together as a family, and see how that feels.

- Do you have a rhythm to your day, week, month? Do you have any loving rituals you could add into your lives, such as lighting a candle and saying a blessing at meals or before bed?

- How is your community support system? If you don't have a good community for yourself or your children, what is one thing you can do to increase that kind of support?

- Do you have time in your family life to play? Are your lives really structured? Does your schedule include time for you to play, too?

Chapter Two

Challenges to Nurturing Relationships

Where Do We Get Stuck When Trying to Nurture Relationships?

As conscious parents, we all want to nurture our relationships. We want our relationships with our children to bring us joy. But somehow day-to-day parenting leaves most of us feeling stressed and tired. Let's look at some of the reasons we may be struggling more than necessary, shine some light on what gets in the way of nurturing our relationships with our children, and learn what we can do about these obstacles.

Our Own Childhood Story

In Book I of the Consciously Parenting Series, we took an in-depth look at our own story (see chapters 5 and 6). We applied Principles 4 (Parent Behavior) and 5 (Interpretation) of consciously parenting as we began to understand that our own early life experiences have a profound influence over how we parent our own children. Our own patterns of attachment and the story of our own experiences can make it easier or more challenging to choose connection when we're at one of the forks in the road.

Let's take a look at a real-life example. Joe grew up in a house where respect was paramount. He was taught to say please and thank you and to respect his elders. He was expected to do what he was told without hesitation. He also often felt that his parents had no idea how he was feeling or what he needed. When Joe had a child of his own, he quickly discovered that he had little tolerance for his son, Jake, not following his orders. On the one hand, Joe understood that he wanted to parent consciously and that children do not always do what they're asked to do. He really wanted to be mindful of Jake's needs. But when Jake refused to do something he was told, Joe's heart would start to pound, and he would feel his anger start to rise. More than anything, he wanted to respond with love and connection, but he often felt like that was the last thing he was capable of doing.

At fork-in-the-road points such as those Joe was facing, we can connect in the emotional space between us and our children. We're not in a state of calm, but we're also not in survival mode, either. In Book I, this state is referred to as "the yellow-light state" on the brain-states stoplight.[3] We still

---

[3] Survival mode is the red-light state, and a state of calm is the green-light state.

can choose how to respond if we can remember to slow down in that moment and pause before acting. For Joe, pausing was an important first step to remember when he made a request of his son.

When Joe wasn't in the middle of a situation that made his heart pound, he took the time to write about his early experiences and to talk with his wife, Jennie, about what it was like for him when he was little. He was able to invite Jennie to come to visit his world, where he could share what it was like for him when he was told to do something by his parents.[4] As he shared his own story with Jennie, he was able to feel what it must be like for Jake when Joe was telling him what to do. He was able to see that he had other choices, including making a request rather than a demand, and that he could share part of his own childhood story with Jake.

After all of this reflection, one night he asked Jake to take out the trash. Jake said, "Why?" Joe was able to pause momentarily before he felt his face grow hot and realize that his heart was pounding. Even though he blurted out, "Because I said so!" he then stopped himself.

"I'm sorry, Jake," he said. "It's really hard for me when you don't just do what I say. When I was your age, I wasn't allowed to say anything besides, 'Yes, sir,' or I was hit. I'm really working to change my patterns here and have this be more respectful for both of us. So I'm making a request that you take out the trash. Would you be willing to take the trash out for us?" Jake understood what his dad was saying and agreed to take out the trash. As he was pulling the trash out of the trash can, Joe asked Jake if he'd ever heard of "Sarah Cynthia Sylvia Stout, Who Would Not Take the Garbage Out," a poem by Shel Silverstein. Joe began to recite the poem, chuckling all the while, as Jake actually did take out the garbage.

---

[4] Relationship therapists Hedy and Yumi Schleifer call this kind of story sharing "crossing the bridge."

Chapter Two

It took a few weeks of really being mindful, but Joe was able to change his pattern around situations when Jake said no or did anything other than fully agree with something Joe asked him to do.

Our Child's Story

Sometimes our child's story shows up and gets in the way of creating a strong connection, and our efforts to nurture the relationship are stymied because we don't understand what our child is communicating through his behaviors. This was the case for Bennie, aged eighteen months, and his mother, Katie. Bennie had a horrible time every time he needed to get dressed, kicking and screaming in a way that confused Katie. The most difficult transition for them both was bath time, which was a total nightmare because Bennie had to get undressed, into the bath, and then out of the bath and into his pajamas. Each step of this process was a fight for Katie, and she was at the end of her rope when she called me.

I asked Katie to tell me the story of Bennie's life, beginning at conception. Katie told me that during the pregnancy, her marriage was difficult and that Bennie had had a long, difficult birth. The umbilical cord had been wrapped tightly around his neck and slowed his descent through the birth canal considerably. Lots of extra interventions had been used to help the baby out. Since birth, Bennie had not liked anything to touch his neck, but he especially didn't like anything going tightly over his head. I wondered if what happened during his birth was part of what he was showing with his aversion to dressing.

I applied the story-sharing work of counselors Ray Castellino and Mary Jackson, from our *Little People, Big Challenges* series of recorded interviews (See Resources for more information), to guide her through the process of helping Bennie to integrate his birth story.

I suggested that Katie tell Bennie the story of his birth when it was time for his bath. She did, and afterward Bennie stared into his mother's eyes in deep silence. For her part, Katie realized she had a much better understanding of Bennie's reactions to dressing and undressing. Now, more aware of what Bennie had been through and was reliving every time he got dressed, she gently placed his clothes over his head, reminding him that he was safe. Within a week or two of Katie sharing his story with him and watching his responses, nurturing him all the while, Bennie was able to get dressed without a struggle.

Shock and Trauma

When overwhelming events happen in our lives or our children's lives, whether prenatally or well after birth, our ability to easily nurture our relationships becomes compromised. We'll be exploring the long-term effects of shock and trauma on relationships in *Healing Connection*, Book IV of the Consciously Parenting Series, as understanding the impact of shock and trauma is critical to healing relationships.

Basically, when we've experienced an overwhelming event—such as an overwhelming birth experience, a cancer diagnosis or treatment, a loss through death or divorce, or a car accident—our bodies and minds go into an old survival pattern. When we're in a survival state (a red-light state), we're in a self-protective mode, and we are unable to really see anyone else.

After my baby, Jacob, died at birth, I was in shock for quite a while, and I lacked the skills and understanding needed to really support myself and to reach out in the way I needed to. I didn't understand how my previous experiences of shock and trauma came together in a perfect storm. I wanted to connect deeply and be there for my nearly four-year-old son, who was experiencing his own shock and trauma from the experience.

But when we as parents are in the midst of our own shock and trauma, it is nearly impossible for us to fully support our children in the way we'd like to, let alone to be able to think clearly enough to solve problems or develop creative solutions to our challenges. If you're so immersed in your own world that you can't really see anyone else, your reactions at forks in the road are more likely to cause disconnection than connection. Creativity, problem solving, and connecting at the fork in the road become possible only when we take time to care for ourselves and allow others to care for us. Even if we cannot directly address the shock and trauma immediately, we can start our own healing process by making an effort to connect with others. It is only then that we can begin to really see our children and what they need in the midst of everything else. See the section called, "What You Can Do About It" for more information about resolving shock and trauma, along with other self-care practices.

When our child has experienced shock or trauma, she is likely to also be in survival mode. Chances are high that she will be difficult to connect with. Perhaps she is acting out to try to get your attention (not in the negative way we always interpret our children's behaviors when they are acting out, but because she really, truly needs to get your attention to survive). Or maybe she is shut down and not engaging with you when you try to connect with her. When a child is screaming most of the day, you probably don't feel like connecting much, and a terrible cycle of disconnection begins.

When we begin to understand that shock and trauma may be playing a role in our child's behaviors, we can begin to shift our own thoughts and feelings, which will then begin to shift the way we're interacting with our child. If you believe you or your child has experienced a shock or trauma, please seek support from someone trained to support families in resolving shock and trauma. (See the resources section in the back of this book.)

Rigid Parental Expectations

Having a parenting philosophy that can guide your parenting choices can truly be a wonderful thing. Most of us need to have a direction to aim for and an understanding of what kinds of parent behaviors will support us in raising a healthy family. However, when the parenting philosophy becomes more important than anything else, it can create more disconnection in our relationship at the fork in the road.

Let's take the philosophy of attachment parenting as an example. One of the guiding principles of attachment parenting is meeting our child's nighttime needs. If we've interpreted that to mean that we cannot have a secure attachment if our child isn't sharing our bed at night, yet we hate sharing sleep, we've missed the attachment boat. If our understanding of something we've read gets in the way of actually connecting with our child, it isn't doing us any good. If sharing sleep works for you and your child, it can be a beautifully connecting experience for everyone. But if it doesn't work and you keep doing it anyway, it isn't going to help you or your child.

One mother of four shared this story of learning to follow her baby's cues despite how they differed from her own expectations. Rae was a very young mother when she had her first daughter. During her daughter's first year, Rae learned about attachment parenting, and it really resonated with her. Shared sleep was something she wanted to try, but her child was already happily sleeping in her crib in another room. When Rae became pregnant with her second child, she looked forward to really connecting with her baby by sharing sleep. However, when her second daughter, Amanda, arrived, neither Rae nor Amanda was able to sleep when they were in the same bed or even the same room. In fact, Amanda slept far better in her own room in her own crib, much to Rae's dismay.

Rae felt it was incredibly important to meet her daughter's nighttime needs. But if she had insisted that Amanda sleep in her bed with her, their relationship would have suffered.

So she instead did everything she could to be available for her daughter if Amanda woke during the night. Because Rae stayed flexible, she and Amanda together were able to find a sleeping arrangement that worked best for both of them and that strengthened their connection. (As an aside, Rae's next two children were both great co-sleepers.)

No matter how much we like a particular parenting philosophy, we're much more likely to end up disconnected than connected with our children if that philosophy leads us to have rigid expectations about what our children are supposed to do. When we can really listen to ourselves and our children, we're more likely to tailor our parental behaviors to our children's individual needs and so create connection.

"Norms" and "Expert" Behavior-Focused Parenting Advice

"Everyone knows that children need to get rid of their bottles and pacifiers before eighteen months!" "If your child won't sleep, just let them cry-it-out!" "The naughty chair is necessary to correct children's behavior." "You can't breastfeed for more than a year!" "Just follow my three simple steps to . . ."

As parents, we're bombarded with advice from every direction—about everything from what our children "should" be doing at a certain chronological age to behavior-focused parenting advice, such as giving children time-outs or anything that is meant to make behaviors go away without looking at their root cause. It can become overwhelming to decide the best path to take.

When our attention turns from the child we have in front of us and the feelings we have about how our child is doing and what our child needs, we are much more likely to choose disconnection at the fork in the road. One-size-fits-all suggestions don't work long-term, nor do they create connection. These are externally based solutions when what you need is an inside job.

What Can You Do About Disconnection?

A powerful and critical first step to creating a change is to recognize that we are moving down a path of disconnection. Without awareness, we cannot begin to make a change. After we have the awareness, we often wonder what else we can do to help support ourselves and our families.

Begin with focusing on yourself. Change must begin with the parents, because the parents are creating the space for the family. Ideally, both parents would find ways to support themselves in their own healing journey, as well as to connect deeply as a couple. For single parents, it is important to make sure you have sufficient support, which includes time by yourself as well as time to connect with others who are supportive in your life. The more that you are able to connect with yourself and with others to heal, the more likely you are to choose the path of connection at the fork in the road and the less likely that you'll find yourself often on a red-light, survival state!

Mindfulness practices can be a wonderful way of creating more emotional space for connection, so you can nurture the relationships with those you love. Some parents find meditation to be a great resource. Others need to move their bodies to clear their minds; those parents may find yoga or tai chi helpful.

Many parents find deep soul writing, a meditative process akin to journaling and explained by Janet Conner in her book *Writing Down Your Soul,* to be helpful in clearing their minds and finding creative solutions to their parenting challenges. Some families have found the work of Dr. Dan Siegel to be very helpful, particularly his work regarding Mindsight. On his website, Mindsight Institute (mindsightinstitute.com), there is a course called "Mindsight for Everyday Life" that is available to the general public. "Mindsight" focuses on techniques that increase self-awareness and can be done from the comfort of home on your own computer.

Because much of our own shock and trauma are held in our bodies, we need to nurture our own bodies so that we can nurture our children. Massage is easily the most available body-work modality and needs to be viewed as a necessity, rather than a luxury, especially when we're having difficulty nurturing our children. Massage releases oxytocin and other stress-inhibiting hormones, which helps us increase our capacity to connect lovingly with our children. If you have a partner, even having your partner give you a hand or foot massage can go a long way towards calming your stress.

In addition to massage, there are many other hands-on bodywork modalities that you may be able to find in your local community, depending on where you live. Some of the modalities that my clients have found helpful include Jin Shin Jyutsu or Jin Shin Tara, the latter of which deals specifically with the resolution of shock from the body; cranial sacral therapy, a gentle hands-on treatment used with everyone from newborns to adults to gently support the body in releasing stored traumas; and the Masgutova Method, which supports the integration of reflexes in children and adults. If they seem interesting to you, it might be worth seeing what you can find near you. Look around your community and maybe you'll find something else that speaks to you.

Regardless of which bodywork modality you choose, developing a plan to release your own stored shock and trauma from your physical body will help you to be more fully present with your children and open up more possibilities for creating connection and nurturing the parent-child relationship!

In our next chapter, we'll be taking a look at how we can begin to nurture our children through the expression of their feelings, especially when we may not have had that experience growing up.

Questions to Ponder

- Where do you get stuck trying to nurture relationships?

- Consider writing your own childhood story, then share it with your partner or a willing friend. If you have a partner, ask your partner to share his or her childhood story with you, even if you think you already know it.

- Consider writing your child's story and share it with your partner or friend, even if they already know the story. Begin sharing the story with your child in small pieces, to build connection. (If you need more support with this step, feel free to contact me.)

- Can you identify any experiences of shock or trauma in your own life? Your partner's life? Your child's life? If so, what is one thing you'd like to do to begin the healing process?

Chapter Three

Handling Feelings: Our Own
and Our Child's

Regulating Our Own Feelings

Feelings have not been easy for me. When I was growing up, my feelings generally weren't validated or respected. It wasn't that my parents set out to invalidate my feelings; it was just that they didn't know how to validate my feelings, most likely because their parents didn't know how to validate their feelings either. Many times I was not aware of my feelings, though I could easily tell how everyone else in my house was feeling at any given moment.

Our early experiences with feelings have a profound effect on how we handle our feelings as adults and how we handle our children's feelings. It is essential that we learn to understand our own feelings, to handle what is ours, and to learn to be present for our children's feelings. Nurturing relationships depends upon supporting each other in the authentic expression of our feelings. This doesn't mean that we dramatize our feelings, but rather that we allow for the natural release of feelings. After talking with hundreds of parents, I have come upon only a handful of people whose parents supported the expression of their feelings. Most reported that it wasn't all right for them, as children, to express their feelings, but their parents were allowed to express the full emotional range. Some people reported having one parent who was able to support the expression of their feelings; others reported that only sadness or only anger were tolerated, while other feelings weren't allowed.

One mom, Roberta, came from a very chaotic childhood, in which only her mother was allowed to have and express feelings. Roberta had little awareness of her own feelings and almost no awareness of her body. This became clear as she described a recent situation in which she had suddenly exploded "without warning." It had scared her, and she wanted to figure out why that had happened.

As we talked about her experiences, growing up and with her current family, it became obvious that pressure was building and building in her like a volcano, but she was completely unaware of it until she was blowing her top. In her experience, the eruption of anger seemed to come completely out of nowhere. Her children, conversely, were very aware of how she was doing before she exploded. In fact, her oldest child, at age twelve, had gotten into the habit of fixing her mom a cup of chamomile tea when Roberta was starting to seem stressed out. The tea being made was often the first clue Roberta had that she was not doing well.

Many people talk about feelings as if they are feeling them when what they're actually doing is thinking. Feelings are actually felt senses in the body. Many of our common expressions come from this fact, such as, "He's a pain in the neck." But many of us are disconnected from our bodies and what they are trying to tell us at any given moment. When we take the time and reconnect with our bodies, we can learn a lot about what we need at any given time. **Being connected with our own felt-sense feelings is vital for being able to connect with the feelings of another person.**

In my discussion with Roberta, I had her reconnect with a stressful situation she had experienced. Because of our mind's ability to time travel, we can think about an experience, and our brain really doesn't know the difference between actually being in it and the memory of being in it. I guided Roberta back through a situation from earlier in the week, one that had ended with her having a meltdown.

As she connected with her body, paying special attention to any areas of tension, pain, or discomfort, she realized that, throughout the day, her body had been sending her signals to tell her that things weren't right. By the time she had reached meltdown status, she had been having physical signs and symptoms for several hours but had been unaware of them.

What would it have looked like if Roberta had handled her situation differently? As Roberta relived the situation, I gave her tips for handling it differently than she had the first time. Her first stressor was seeing that one of her children had made a big mess in the kitchen and left it sitting out. I suggested that Roberta, upon seeing the mess, take a deep breath. She could then connect with her body and notice areas of tension in her shoulders, particularly her right shoulder. The body is very literal. A feeling in the shoulder represents shouldering respon-sibility, and the right side of the body is associated with anger. So in that moment, she was angry about shouldering the respon-sibility of the mess she saw in the kitchen.

I recommended that she breathe into the feeling of pain in her shoulder and acknowledge what her body was telling her that she was feeling. I suggested that she place a hand on the spot that was hurting as she did. She acknowledged out loud that she had been feeling angry because everything always seemed to be landing on her shoulders.

Sometimes parents need to say their feelings out loud; other times they need to share their feelings with someone who can hear them (though, at this point, not their child), or they need to write about their feelings. This is especially true if feeling their feelings is new to them. If they have been getting in touch with their felt-sense feelings for a while, sometimes just quietly acknowledging how they are feeling is enough. Remember that emotion is energy in motion, and the feelings need an avenue of expression. Whether that means we talk, yell, find something to safely hit, cry, or go for a long run, energy needs to be moved through in a way that doesn't hurt anyone, including ourselves.

Next, after feeling and expressing her feeling in some way, depending upon the strength of the feeling, Roberta needed to calm herself down. Parents who are not usually in touch with their bodies and how they're feeling often need to make a con-scious effort to return to a state of calm after feeling a feeling. Sometimes returning to a calm state requires the assistance of a therapist. Other times, if a parent has a prayer or meditation practice, doing this practice will help. Some parents have sooth-ing music they listen to that helps them to calm down. Other parents have a friend or spouse who can simply breathe with them or hold them until they learn how to regulate their breath-ing for themselves. Remember, if we didn't learn the process of emotional regulation when we were growing up with our own parents (and we haven't had any experiences with someone helping us to regulate as an adult), we cannot teach it to our children. Roberta was able to use her husband as a support to calm herself down because they had a great connection. She called him on the phone at work, and he was able to talk to her softly, which helped her to calm herself.

Only once we, the parent, are more regulated (out of the red-light state) is it time to decide on an action step. Feelings are communications from our bodies and spirits that something isn't right in our world and some action needs to be taken. But it is vital that we take this action only when we are more regulated, or we will not make good decisions and are likely to hurt someone. At the same time, if we are extremely rational and in our heads, we aren't going to be connecting emotionally with our children. We need to be in a state of relative calm so that we can respond with love to our children, rather than being in a red-light state and reacting out of our own pain. When we value our own feelings and their expression in ways that respect those around us, we are modeling that behavior for our children.

After Roberta reconnected with her husband over the phone, she was feeling less overwhelmed. She went back into the kitchen and took in the scenery. Yes, there were dishes everywhere. She felt the familiar tension in her shoulder and knew that she needed to take action. She called her children into the kitchen and asked them to tell her what they could see. She guided them through the process of locating the things that needed to be fixed and helped them to clean up the mess they had left. She shared how she felt when they left the kitchen like this and how it was important that everyone work together. (It is important that she didn't just tell them what to do, but explained how their actions affected her. This is the essence of connection at the fork in the road. It isn't devoid of our feelings.) In her case, her children weren't unreasonable, and they cleaned up once they realized what needed to be done. They just didn't realize they had left the mess or how their mom was feeling about it.

The next time I spoke to Roberta, she talked about how much more aware she was of her own body, and how if she started to feel tension in her body, she was much more aware of it long before she actually reached the point of exploding. It wasn't that she never exploded again, but that her awareness of herself increased. It was a beautiful step for her. And as a result of it, her children began to feel safer with her, especially because she shared part of her own story with them: about how she didn't have good body awareness and didn't know when she was starting to get upset. They were allowed to be part of the process of naming what they were seeing from their mom, so the process felt less out of control for them. Over time, there was a lot more trust between Roberta and her kids, not because Roberta became a perfect mom, but because her kids knew they could talk to her about what was happening.

Steps for Handling Our Own Feelings:

1. Connect with the physical body and the felt sensations.

2. Feel and express the feeling in some way.

3. Regulate yourself, with or without assistance, depending upon your needs and past experiences.

4. Decide what action to take. (Remember that feelings are telling you some action needs to be taken.)

5. Take action.

Handling Our Child's Feelings

If, when we were children, our feelings were not valued, we may struggle with our own children's feelings in the present time. We may intend to accept their feelings, but find ourselves trying to shut down the feelings, as happened to us in our past with our own parents. This is especially true when our children have very strong feelings and when they seem to be expressing those feelings toward us after we've done something they perceive as wrong.

As we are working to change our patterns regarding our feelings, our growing children are going to give us many opportunities to really understand how we feel about our own feelings. How you typically react to your child's feelings will tell you a lot about how your feelings were normally handled when you were growing up. Many parents react in one of the following two ways:

Shut down all feelings other than happiness. If your feelings were shut down as a child, you may simply not allow your child to express feelings. This might mean that when your child expresses a feeling, you find yourself telling her that she doesn't really feel that way, sending your child to his room until he is done feeling the feeling, or even joking to make her move out of her feeling state.

Stop the feeling and expression of selected feelings. In this case, there may be individual feelings, like anger or sadness, that you do not tolerate well. When these feelings arise in your child, you may find yourself resorting to strategies to make the feelings stop.

We cannot be present for someone else's feelings if we have difficulty handling our own feelings. So in order to acknowledge and change our patterns, we need to repeat the steps for handling our own feelings.

We are also more likely to invalidate our child's feelings when we are overwhelmed by our own feelings. When we invalidate our child's feelings, we are teaching them to disconnect from their own internal guidance system—the very thing they need most to navigate out in the world as adults.

Teaching the Language of Feelings

We need to actively teach our children feeling words by modeling. In other words, we need to show them what we are feeling, and we need to name those feelings. When our children are expressing feelings, naming what we are seeing them express is very helpful for them. With older children, you might try describing what you see and then ask, "Are you feeling _____?"

For example, Sherry noticed that her son was stomping his foot on the ground while his face was scrunched up around his nose. She told him what she was observing and said, "I'm wondering if you're feeling frustrated right now." This gave him the opportunity to connect with what he was expressing and see if it matched the words mom had just given him.

With younger children or those not well versed in the language of feelings, give them the five main feeling words— *mad, glad, sad, scared,* and *happy*—to help them start developing a vocabulary for describing feelings. When you see someone on television or someone in your life who is expressing a feeling, break down the visual observation for your child and ask if she knows the feeling. The more you incorporate a vocabulary of feeling words into real life, the more it will stick, and the more you'll be able to communicate about feelings—yours and your child's—in a healthy way.

Chapter Three

Feelings, Nurturing, and the Stoplight Brain States

In chapter two, I mentioned the brain-states stoplight, a concept from Book I of the Consciously Parenting Series. On this stop-light, the green light is a calm and regulated state, the yellow light is a more emotional state, and the red light is a state of survival. As we experience parenting situations at the fork in the road where we have a choice between nurturing connection or creating disconnection in the parent-child relationship, we need to remember that either our child or we, the parent, or both of us, is in an emotional place. When your son stops cooperating and is agitated, when your daughter is beginning to get really excited about her grandma coming to visit, they slip out of the green-light brain state and into the yellow. When our child starts to show the early warning signs of a yellow-light state, we can nurture connection by connecting with our child's feelings and eventually helping him return to a state of calm (a green light).

What are the early warning signs that a child is no longer in a complete state of calm? Does your child start to move her body, twirling in circles or fidgeting? Do you see signs of distress on his face? Does he refuse to cooperate? Is he not getting along with friends? Does she start calling someone a name? Does he take something away from another child? Does she stop talking and hold very still?

Pay attention to your child's early warning signs and realize that you are sitting at the fork in the road. Which direction will you choose to go? How will you choose connection in this moment?

Show Love or Teach a Lesson?

"But Rebecca," many parents say to me, "I don't always feel like nurturing my child! If you could see what she was doing, you'd understand why I cannot respond with love, compassion, and nurturing. She needs to learn that her behavior is unacceptable."

There are going to be situations where we don't feel like responding to our children with love. Instead, we feel that it is time to teach our children a lesson. They've gotten us really upset, or embarrassed us, or brought out a part of us that we don't like.

We need to understand that these situations and these feelings are not accidental or out of the blue, even if they feel that way in the moment. These are opportunities from our own past— perhaps from our childhoods or maybe from a more recent, adult-age relationship challenge—to see our current relationships more clearly.

When you stop and think about it, are you perhaps reacting to your child in the same way that your parents reacted to you when you did something similar? What did you need as a child? What if your parents had known about the power of nurturing and the importance of recognizing that all behavior is a communication of unmet needs? How would that have felt to you? Would you have been more likely to do what they wanted you to do if they had listened to you and acknowledged you and your feelings?

When we feel frustrated or angry with our child in a particular situation, that feeling is about us—not our child. We need to recognize and then validate our own feelings about the situation. ("I'm feeling really frustrated because she won't just let me brush her teeth! How hard is that? All she has to do is open her mouth, and I do the rest!") We can't take in someone else's feelings and connect with them unless we have first connected with our own feelings. It is even better if you can share your feelings with someone else—someone who can hear you without trying to judge you or fix it for you.

After a parent's feelings have been validated, I often suggest that he or she spend some time writing about the situation. It is amazing what happens when you go back through a situation and write out exactly what happened (as if you are reliving it in slow motion). What happened first? What happened next?

How was everyone feeling? Do you notice any stoplight changes happening with either you or your child?

Then let your writing rest for a day or so. After you haven't read it for at least twenty-four hours, go back and read it with new eyes. Many times, it becomes apparent what your beliefs are or where you are getting stuck. Sometimes even a situation from your past, in which you felt the same way as you did in the situation with your child, will come to the surface. This type of writing has been a very powerful tool in my own life. When you're in the midst of a parenting challenge, you often don't see the clues to your healing moments when they are right in front of you.

Once you have worked through your own reaction, have validated your own feelings, and perhaps gained some understanding about yourself, then go back and look at your child's behavior again with new eyes. What did your child need? What was she (unconsciously) trying to communicate to you with her behavior? What could you have done to connect?

Our children need to be taught appropriate behaviors, but they are also learning how to handle conflicts by how we choose to handle our conflicts with them. When everyone is in a green-light state, you can talk about appropriate ways of getting needs met. ("I know that when you started pulling on my shirt that you needed my attention. Next time, could you use your words to let me know that you need my full attention? Maybe we could practice that so that we both know what that might look and feel like.")

A Real-Life Example of Handling Feelings: Ours and Theirs (Courtesy of My Own Children)

Many times, the biggest difference between behavior-focused and relationship-centered solutions is the implementation. In behavior-focused parenting, there are consequences for a child's behavior, but consequences don't create more connection in the relationship.

For example, how many times have our children exhibited "difficult" behaviors in the car when we are driving somewhere? Sometimes these behaviors can be dangerous, because they distract us from being able to pay attention to the road. Ignoring such disruptions isn't really an option. But it is possible to handle them in a way that creates connection and shows our children how we would like them to be able to handle life's inevitable upsets.

When I was growing up, my parents did a lot of yelling when my brothers were disruptive in the car. They tried putting physical barriers such as coolers in between my brothers, but my brothers merely saw the coolers as a challenge to overcome as they continued to bother each other. Sometimes the car would come to a screeching halt. One time, in total desperation, my mom made one of my brothers get out and walk for a mile because he just wouldn't calm down. When I became a parent and began having difficulty in the car with my own two boys, I would often pull the car over so that I could yell at them. That was the type of reaction I had seen growing up. Yelling and consequences were the only tools my parents had to try to regain control in a situation in which they felt completely out of control. So for a long time, those were the only tools that I had with my own children. I knew they didn't really work. We were all more upset than when the disruptions first started, but I wasn't sure what else to do.

Most of us grew up with consequences being doled out for our missteps—usually with a side of anger, shame, or disappointment thrown in for good measure, to make sure we learned our lesson. I've since learned that lessons are learned best when everyone is calm, though I had never seen my own parents discipline us when they were calm.

It was a journey in every sense of the word for me to move away from just reacting to my children's behaviors and my own sense of powerlessness and into realizing that I could, indeed, make situations different by responding with love and to the relationship. I became empowered by small successes where I was able to use loving influence and keep everyone's needs in mind to make changes.

When I began to shift my understanding of how I was interacting with my children—and realizing that my reactions were only adding to their dysregulation—I started looking more at what everyone needed when we were in the car together. I needed to be safe. I needed it to be peaceful in the car. I needed my children to get along well enough for us to reach our destination without us all becoming totally frustrated—or worse.

I had to recognize first and foremost that I was the one who was most upset by their behavior. It was I who couldn't concentrate. Sometimes they were having loud fun, but sometimes there was fighting going on.

I also needed to calm myself down before I did anything. First, I pulled the car over to the side of the road, without yelling or squealing the tires to let my sons know just how serious I felt the situation really was. Then I took a few deep breaths. I was careful not to blame them. Whatever I felt was *my* feeling. It was triggered by what was going on with them, but it was mine. I would then remind myself that I was the parent and that I could make this situation different.

Once I was feeling a little calmer, I spoke to my children. I stated the obvious: "I am having a hard time concentrating with the fighting going on in the back seat. I'm not sure that this is working for either of you. Let's work together and find a way to make this work for everyone."

The first time I said this, my kids stared at me blankly from the backseat, as if their real mother had been kidnapped by aliens. I guess being talked to this way was radically different for them, which actually made me feel somewhat sad.

My feelings then told me that there needed to be an action next. I asked my boys how we could make this situation work better for everyone, since they were old enough to handle such a question.

"He keeps touching me! I keep telling him to stop, but he won't!"

"He took my toy away and won't give it back!"

I took another deep breath to calm my nervous system and return myself to my conscious, rational, thinking brain. I turned around to face them and look at their precious little faces.

"It sounds like you're having a difficult time today in the car."

"Well, he..."

"I know it is frustrating to always have someone touching you or taking away your toys. I wonder if you're feeling angry right now."

"It is frustrating, and I am angry! Why can't he..."

"We all have angry feelings sometimes. They tell us that something needs to change."

I put my hand on my chest and said, "My goodness, my heart is beating really fast. Sometimes when I'm having big feelings, my heart beats very fast. I wonder if your hearts are beating fast, too?"

They put their hands on their chests and felt their hearts beating fast. I told them that I was going to concentrate on my breathing to make mine slow down and wondered if they wanted to do that, too. They did and started focusing on their own breathing and their heartbeats.

"Mine is going slower now," reported one of my sons from the back seat.

The other piped in, "Mine, too!"

"Now that our hearts are beating slower, we're more able to think about how we can make this better. I'm wondering if either of you have an idea for how we could make our car ride more pleasant so that we can get to the park as soon as possible and you can both get out and play."

After a short discussion, my older son moved into the front seat, and we put on a Jim Weiss audio story to play in the background. We then headed back onto the road with everyone happy and regulated.

Did I tolerate the unacceptable behavior? No. Did I have a mommy fit over it? No. I modeled regulation, problem-solving, and caring about everyone's needs.

It took a lot practice for me to change my reactions. And sometimes I still fall back into my old pattern of just telling my sons what they were doing wrong and what consequence I was going to be giving them for their misbehavior. There are times when I get really mad and don't act like a conscious parent. When that happens, I work to forgive myself, recognizing that I am actually creating new neural pathways in my brain as I change my behavior. This type of change requires time and patience, but eventually interacting with my children this way has become my normal reaction. Every time my children say something, I see that I have a choice about how I respond. Every time I speak to them is an opportunity to connect or not.

We Always Have a Choice

It is so easy to fall into giving our children consequences to change their behavior. Counting to three, which is an everyday parenting tool for most parents, including me for a long time, and threatening them with a timeout or other punishment are all our attempts to control our child's behavior. When we are resorting to these behavior-focused techniques, we are feeling out of control ourselves. We have needs that aren't being met. But it isn't our child's job to meet our needs. We need to take responsibility for our own feelings and actions so that our children can learn to do the same.

Consciously parenting means that sometimes we need to work harder than others to parent out of the present moment rather than reacting from all those other times that our children didn't listen to us or that we weren't listened to as children.

Questions to Ponder

- What feelings are you comfortable expressing by yourself? With others?

- What feelings were you allowed to express growing up?

- What feelings were other family members allowed to express when you were growing up?

- What feelings are you comfortable with your child expressing?

- What feelings are challenging for you to witness when your child is expressing them?

Chapter Four

Communication: Verbal and Nonverbal

Verbal Communication: The Words We Choose

"Make my words tender and sweet, for tomorrow I may have to eat them."

This saying is never more true than in parenting. We do eat our words. And we have them come back up again daily as our children parrot them back to us. The words we choose can make a difference in the level of cooperation we get from our children. Even more important is recognizing the feeling behind the words we choose. That feeling makes a big difference between connection and disconnection.

Japanese researcher Masaru Emoto has taken pictures of water crystals that formed after different words were either spoken into a full water bottle or written on a piece of paper that was taped onto the bottle. He has published his water-crystal pictures in several books, including *The Hidden Messages in Water*. One shows pictures of water that had been imbued with the messages "Do it now!" and "Let's do it." The crystals from the water bottle with "Do it now!" inscribed on the side are ugly and blackened. The crystals formed from the water with "Let's do it" written on the outside of the container are white and have a beautiful, snowflake-like structure.

When I first saw these photos, I thought about how much water our bodies are made of. What happens to the water that makes up our bodies when we use ugly words, like the command "Do it now!" toward ourselves or toward our children? I was also struck by the difference the word *let's* made. It changes the message entirely, and is a word we can easily incorporate into the daily language we use with our children.

When we are irritated with our children, we need to recognize that part of this irritation is our responsibility. We are responsible for our own feelings and our own reactions to our children. Our parenting vocabulary usually comes from our parents' mouths, which sometimes works beautifully. But sometimes things that our parents (or other caregivers) said to us were hurtful, and now, when we say them to our children, they are just as hurtful.

As children, we deserved to be respected. We deserved to be valued and to have our feelings respected. We may feel that our children deserve this too, but find ourselves talking to them in a way that is not respectful. When we haven't experienced those positive words in our own lives, how can we be expected to use them with our children?

Being aware that our words can tell children what we expect of them is of vital importance. For example, when we say, "He's not a good sleeper," we are telling our child that he's not a good sleeper and probably won't become one. If we say that he needs extra help settling down during the night, it opens the possibility for him to start sleeping better.

Nonviolent Communication and Learning New Words

New tools are very important if we want to make changes in our language. Nonviolent communication (NVC), developed by psychologist Marshall Rosenberg, offers some of the best, most powerful tools I've found for creating those positive changes in the language we use with our families. In NVC, the emphasis is on teaching us communication skills that we can take into our relationships—all of them—including how to use different words to express our needs.

My colleague Stephanie Mattei teaches NVC classes, and one of the most life-changing lessons she's given me was about the difference between a need and a strategy. I often found myself saying to my children, "I need you to pick up your socks." In Stephanie's class, I learned that these words weren't express-ing my need, but rather were a strategy that I was using to get my need met. My real need was for order in my home. A strategy for meeting that need was to get my son to pick up his socks. Every-one has needs, and everyone's needs are important. There are many strategies that can be used to meet needs. It isn't just one solution, like what I had been saying about the socks.

So, in my example, I might express my need: "I have a need for order in the home." My kids would probably stare blankly at me again, figuring that the alien was back. Then I could say, "I'm wondering if you would be willing to pick up your socks?"

"No. I really don't want to pick up my socks right now," one of them might respond.

"Would you be willing to talk about how we can meet my need for order in the home? I'm wondering what you need right now?"

"I'm home from school, and this is my play time. I want to play!"

"What if we made cleaning up a game? Would you be willing to do that?"

"What kind of game?"

We would be able to talk it out and find a solution that worked for everyone—and one that kept everyone's needs in mind. We would set a timer and make cleaning up a race. In the end, the house would be clean, and my sons would have had fun. Win-win.

According to the basic premises of NVC, there is never a conflict at the level of need. There are only conflicts at the level of strategy. When we take the time to discover what our own core needs are in a given situation and to identify the core needs of our children, we can then find strategies that meet the needs of everyone.

Most of us aren't aware of our needs or what needs truly are. Inbal Kashtan, of Bay NVC, an NVC group in San Francisco, has graciously shared the group's list of words describing common human needs, so that we can become familiar with words that describe those needs. For example, if I'm aware that I am having a physical need that isn't being met, I can look in the chart's category on physical needs and find a word that describes my need. Perhaps I have a need for rest, as is common for parents with young children. My child might have a need for autonomy. As I look at the list, the word *choice* resonates with me, so I might ask my child if he needs some more choice.

Connection	Interconnection	Meaning	Peace	Celebration
Acceptance	Belonging	Contribution	Beauty	Joy
Affection	Consideration	Creativity	Communion	Mourning
Appreciation	Cooperation	Hope	Ease	Play
Clarity	Mutuality	Inspiration	Harmony	**Physical Needs**
Communication	Support	Learning	Order	Nourishment
Community	Trust	**Autonomy**	**Honesty**	Rest
Compassion	Power	Choice	Authenticity	Sustenance
Intimacy	**Competence**	Respect	Integrity	Shelter, cover
Love	Effectiveness	Spontaneity	Presence	Touch
Understanding	Growth	Space		

NVC is a communication tool and a great way of understanding what our underlying needs are in our daily lives. When we start understanding our own needs, we can help our children to understand their needs.

To understand how NVC can make a difference in nurturing connection with our family, let's look at another example. Molly, the mother of three children, was feeling really upset that her children weren't doing the housework that she had asked them to do on a regular basis. She found herself increasingly frustrated that she was spending so much of her time cleaning and no one else seemed to be pitching in as much as she was. She found herself yelling very easily at her children, particularly when they were playing and making a mess of any kind. She began to control what they were allowed to play with by forcibly removing the messy toys from her children's hands. When she talked to me about this situation, she was confused about how this had gotten so out of hand and why she was reacting so angrily. She recognized that she was overreacting, but had no idea how to make this different for herself and her children.

Before she could have a constructive conversation with her children, Molly needed to understand a little more about where she was coming from. The first question I asked her was to recall what lessons about cleaning up and playing with messy things she had learned from her own childhood. What had her experience been growing up? As she reflected, she said that her mom had not allowed messes and had often gotten upset at her when she made a mess. She started to cry a little bit as she connected with her own pain from when she was a little girl. She made the connection with her own part in this situation in the present with her children. They were afraid of what she was going to do to them next if they made a mess, just as she had been with her own mother.

I asked her what it does to her when she sees her children making a mess. I told her to imagine that she had just walked into the room where her children were making a mess and to connect with her body in that moment. Did she feel tightness or pain somewhere in her body? She paused for a moment and replied that it made her stomach twist into a knot, her shoulders tighten, and her face feel hot. I told her to stay with those feelings and allow herself to feel them fully. I asked when in the past she had felt those feelings before. She connected fully to those physical feelings, and when she spoke again, she actually sounded like a young child: "Mommy was in a bad mood, and she was yelling at us because we were bad again."

Before Molly could be fully present with her current situation, she had some unfinished business she needed to address and bring into conscious awareness. Her own history and feelings from the past were getting in the way of her ability to see her present situation clearly.

I encouraged her to express her feelings around that childhood event and make connections with her own children and how they must be feeling in the present moment. This was a big aha moment for Molly. She had felt so resentful toward her own mother for not allowing her the space to play and to make a mess, yet she was doing the same thing to her own children. She now understood that her children must feel the same way she had. She was able to step into her children's shoes, which gave her a new perspective on her children's behaviors.

I reminded her that she had a need and that looking at and connecting with where her children were coming from didn't mean that they should just do whatever they wanted and let the house be a wreck. Instead, it meant taking others' needs into consideration, which will help us connect more to our own inner guidance once our feelings have been expressed and are out of the mix.

Because of Molly's early experiences, she also needed some additional assistance setting healthy boundaries with her children—ones that were not too rigid and unreasonably inflexible, but were also not too lenient.

With her new understanding, Molly decided to bring her children together for a family meeting. Because she hadn't had many family meetings, she started off by saying that it was a time to hear everyone's ideas and that she would be starting by bringing up something that was important to her.

She began with something like this: "When I was growing up, my mom felt that keeping a really, really clean house was important and that sometimes it became more important than anything else. I felt awful about how I was treated when I was growing up. I felt like any minute I was going to do something else that upset my mom. I'm wondering if you are feeling that way, too."

Then she opened up space for her children to share their feelings on this topic: "In the past, I don't think I've really made it safe for you to tell me how you are really feeling. I want you to know that it is OK now and that you aren't going to get into trouble for telling me how you have been feeling."

Once she had heard and validated her children's feelings (using words like, "I didn't know it was so hard for you" and "Tell me more about that,") she and her children were able to engage in a conversation about how they can solve this problem together, in a way where everyone's needs are met.

That conversation might have sounded something like this:

Molly: I do really have a need for order in our home. It is so much easier for me to find the things that everyone needs and to keep everything running. What do you each find helpful about it?

Jerry (age twelve): I don't like to clean up. It isn't fun at all.

Molly: Sounds like having fun is important to you.

Jerry: Yes!

Molly: What do you think we could do to make cleaning up more fun? I'd love to hear if you have any ideas about that!

Jerry: Once, a long time ago, we did some races to see how much we could clean up before the timer rang. I think that was back in your Fly Lady days. Do you remember when you used to get those daily emails from Fly Lady, and she'd tell you to drop whatever you were doing and go clean one thing for fifteen minutes? That was fun because it was a challenge.

Molly: That sounds like a great idea!

Seth (age nine): I don't like to race. I'd rather just work on a spot and get it cleaned up. But I don't really like to clean alone. It is boring when I'm all by myself! If you want to clean with me, and we'll just tackle one spot together, I'd be fine with that.

Molly: Thank you for your thoughts, Seth.
Sounds like you have a need for companionship while you are working on a task. I enjoy that as well.

Before Molly started this conversation, she was very clear that she needed help with keeping order in the home. Because she was clear on this need for herself, she had more flexibility with the strategies used by her children, because the most important aspect for her was to feel supported. Had she not been clear on her own needs, she might have felt more restricted to only one specific strategy, such as getting Jerry to take out the garbage three times per week. As it turned out, Jerry was willing to help with the bigger jobs and even willing to take on additional tasks as long as his needs to have fun and be challenged were met.

The first step to changing a family dynamic such as the one in Molly's family is to look inside yourself and understand your own expectations and, if possible, where they came from.

If you are interested in learning more about NVC, check out the information in the resources section for suggested readings, audios, and classes.

Metacommunication: Communicating Beyond Words

Every morning, my son was waking up in a bad mood. He would often start yelling at me or begin to fight with his brother before we had even fully awoken. I truly began to dread the morning and seeing my son. He would wake up and come into the bed where I was sleeping, and I could often feel the negative energy pouring off of him. As I felt this before anyone had said a word,

I would often start to feel very negative and immediately become overwhelmed by the thought of another day starting out badly.

Suddenly, one morning it hit me: He was communicating to me loud and clear with his emotional state and his actions, but what was I communicating to him? I was joining in on his negativity before anyone said a word. Staying in this place of negativity was only keeping us stuck. I was blaming him for the way our day was starting, and I felt like I could do nothing about it. It was only leading to day after day of the same thing.

The words of Anthony Robbins came to mind: "If you do what you've always done, you'll get what you've always gotten." I didn't want more of the same. I was ready for a change.

And then I remembered the words of Gandhi: "Be the change you want to see in the world." If I wished to see a change in my family's world, I needed to be that change.

I decided to try an experiment. The very next day, when my son crawled into bed, I decided to see what a difference I could make without saying a word. I connected with my own feelings first. As he lay in bed next to me, my stomach turned with a feeling of anxiety about what might happen with him next. I was dysregulated to the core! I was not in the present moment. I took some nice deep breaths, said a prayer for peace within myself, and began to envision a different outcome.

I began to shift my own attention to my son—my precious son, whom I had wanted and nursed and held close for years—how awful it must feel for him to wake up that dysregulated. That really must be horrible! I began to think loving thoughts about my son and what I wanted for him in his life: joy and peace, harmony and love. I changed the focus of my attention from what I was afraid would happen next to who my son truly was and what he truly deserved. I shifted only my thoughts and didn't say anything out loud. My son and I both had our eyes closed and were not even facing each other.

And something amazing happened. When my son spoke that morning, he was calm. Wow! It was the first time I had felt hope for a long time. And the rest of our day went much better, too. It wasn't perfect by any stretch, but it was better.

My example is meant to show the power of what we communicate to our kids when we are not even speaking. We know from lots of research (and from lots of experiences) that parents and children, in particular, are very connected with one another and that we do not need words to communicate. In fact, 85 percent of our communication is nonverbal, or meta-communication. So much of how we feel we communicate to our children without words, so imagine how powerful it can be when we do use words!

Everything we communicate to one another through our thoughts, our words, and our actions has the power to create closeness and connection or to create disconnection. What do you choose to create in your relationship today?

We communicate with each other in many ways. When you are beginning to explore the concept of what you are communicating to others beyond your words, you may consider asking a friend, your partner, or your spouse to observe you and (gently) share what they are seeing. Ask them to pay attention to your gestures, the timing of your words, the volume you're using (we get loud when we're not feeling heard), the emotional tone of your words, whether or not you make eye contact and the feeling you're sending with your eyes, the words you are choosing, and your physical proximity to the person you're talking with or to.

To experience what I'm talking about, try this experiment: Say to a friend, "I'm glad to see you." Say it with a smile on your face and see how that feels. Then grit your teeth and say the same words. Next, look your friend in the eyes, connect with how much you enjoy their company, and say those same words. Then look at them, think of a time they did something you didn't enjoy, and say the same words. Next, look away and say the words. Move close to your friend and say them, then move to the other side of the room and repeat. The same words can have many meanings, depending upon how we say them, but *how we feel when we say them* is perhaps even more important than the words themselves!

When our relationship with our child is not going the way we want, we need to recognize that we cannot change another person. But we can look at our own part of our interactions with our child and see if we can make a change. Small changes over time make big changes in relationships! And any change starts with our own awareness of what we're actually communicating.

The next time you are having a moment where things aren't going well, stop and pay attention to how you are feeling. Pay attention to what you are communicating with your nonverbal communication. Consider asking someone else to give you feedback—perhaps an older child, your spouse, or a good friend who can be honest with you about what they are seeing. Ask them to help you see what you are communicating so that you can start to increase your own awareness in these situations and you can start making a change.

When We Know Our Metacommunication Is Negative

Many times, we hold on to our negativity because of how our children's behaviors make us feel. But our children aren't able to change the patterns in our relationship with them. Only we can. And it takes forgiving ourselves and our children to move forward.

"But he's the one who just refused to do what I asked! I didn't do anything wrong here!" is the type of response many parents have.

That may very well be true. But do we want to be right, or do we want to change our relationship with our children? It is our choice. Holding onto negativity only shows our children how to hold onto negativity. Doing something to punish our children for how they have made us feel only teaches them that we can do what we want to them, even hurt them, because we are bigger, stronger, older, or more powerful—and increases disconnection. But if you take responsibility for your part in the relationship, even if it is only 2 percent responsibility, you are showing them how to take responsibility. You are putting the relationship first, and you will be starting to create connection and be a loving influence in your relationship. You are also letting your children know that they are important. The power of love has the ability to move mountains. It is the only thing that can.

When you shift your own negativity, it frees you up to then communicate positively on every level. Pay attention to what *you* are communicating, and you can seize the opportunity to start making your relationship with your children different!

The Importance of Nutrition in Nurturing

There are many foods that are harmful to the body and can alter a child's behavior and ability to remain calm and present. Especially problematic are MSG (monosodium glutamate) and artificial sweeteners, as both are neurotoxins. Examples of artificial sweeteners, which cause similar changes in the brain as MSG, include saccharin (Sweet 'n Low), asparatame (Equal, NutriSweet), and sucralose (Splenda). Russell Blaylock is a physician who has been actively educating parents about the dangers of these substances. They cause changes in the brain.

(continued)

Some children are incredibly sensitive to these substances. Others show no obvious signs of a problem, but the effects are cumulative. You never know how much it is going to take before the child will be affected permanently. The best bet is to avoid these food additives entirely!

The best bet is always to eat whole foods, as close to their natural state as possible. For starters, cook meals at home and offer raw fruits and vegetables as snacks, and limit or avoid foods devoid of nutrients, like chips, crackers, boxed cereals, and other processed foods. Children (and adults) who support their bodies with good food will have better behavior than those who don't. If you notice fluctuations in your children's moods and/or behaviors, keep a food diary. If your child is eating the same processed foods over and over again, it is time to make a change.

Questions to Ponder

- How is your verbal communication with your child? With your partner? Do you have a well-established vocabulary of words that nurture and connect? Or is this an area you need some additional support?

- Did you know that many communities have NVC groups where parents can gather and learn NVC skills? There are also online groups if you'd like to learn more about this tool.

- Consider asking someone to observe your metacommunication with your children or your partner. Are your verbal and your nonverbal communication similar? What can you do to shift the way that you are feeling deep down? What subconscious beliefs show up in the way you move your body?

- Have you considered the role of "artificial foods" in your child's behavior? In your own behavior and moods? Consider writing down what you eat for a day (or a week) and note any connections you see to food and behavior.

Chapter Five

Parental Behaviors for
Nurturing Relationships

Ever been in a situation where your child did something, and
before you knew it, your child was grounded for a week, and
you wondered who was going to be punished more, you or
them? When you look back at these situations, do you not really
remember much about it, but wonder what actually happened?

Maybe it went something like this: It was bedtime, and you were tired. You told your child to go to bed, and he rolled his eyes at you. Oh boy!

You heard the words "Don't you roll your eyes at me!" come rolling off the tongue of someone very nearby, and then you realized it was you saying them!

Your child replied, "Whatever," making you fully angry.

You yelled, "Don't you tell me 'whatever' and roll your eyes at me! I deserve to be respected and that is disrespectful! Go to bed!"

"You can't make me go to bed!"

"Oh, yes I can! If you aren't in bed in thirty seconds, you're grounded for a week!"

Your child stopped and stared at you, then moved to a spot in front of the Xbox to start another video game.

"That's it! You're grounded!"

This is a clear example of a disconnection, and it all happened in the space of less than a minute. You are an intelligent, educated parent whose common sense was hijacked because your child didn't go to bed right when he was asked to go. Your child got really mad at you, but still didn't go to bed, and you are going to have to spend the week together, probably repeating similar occurrences, because of your decisions in that heated moment.

What happened?

Stress and Regression

When we become stressed out, we lose full access to our prefrontal cortex, or our higher rational thinking brain, and other areas of our brain—the ones that aren't responsible for cognitive, rational thought—take over. As we get upset, our emotional brains take charge of our thinking (oh no!). This is a problem, because that part of the brain essentially has an IQ that's 25 points lower than that of our prefrontal cortex, the part of the brain that's active when we're calm. If we drop even further and land in the lowest-functioning area of our brain, the reptilian or survival brain, we lose access to nearly 50 IQ points. Personally, I think that parenting can be challenging enough when we have all of our IQ points! This is why it is important that we refrain from making decisions when we are upset. We don't have access to all of our IQ points and probably aren't going to make the best parenting decisions, as shown in the example above.

Here's another way of looking at these brain states. When we are very reactive, we are probably functioning emotionally like a child between the ages of two and five. How well do two- to five-year-olds evaluate and make decisions? Not so well. They may be able to make a decision based on some of the information, but they are unable to see the big picture. It's not that they are unwilling to see the big picture, but that they are *unable* to do so. When you are reactive, it isn't that you are unwilling to do things differently. In that moment, you are unable to do so. You need to work to calm yourself so that you can return to your chronological age.

When our children are stressed, they also regress emotionally to a younger age. This is part of the reason that your teen probably has moments that remind you of a toddler's meltdowns. Even though they are chronologically older, when teens are stressed out, they may have needs that are closer to those of a toddler, and they may have the corresponding inability to see the big picture and solve problems. It is essential to teach our children about these brain states so that they can learn how to manage theirs when stressful situations happen.

Responding to Developmental Regressions

Growing up is a one step forward, two steps back, followed by three steps forward, experience. From time to time, all children will act younger than their age. This is generally a source of frustration for parents who have the illusion that they've "arrived" now that their children can do "X" on their own.

For example, children may be able to buckle themselves into the car seat and do it for a while, then one day seem unable to do it. As parents, we have a tendency to react to this sort of behavior because we don't understand it. We want our children to be able to continue buckling themselves in, and we know that they know how to do it! After all, they were able to do it yesterday, and there have been no major catastrophes or accidents overnight that would have affected their physical abilities. The situation makes no sense to our adult brains. Pick the buckle up in your hand and click it together. What's so hard about it?

Another example is a child who was previously potty trained beginning to wet himself every day. Or a child suddenly refusing to sleep in her own bed unless a parent is with her. Many times, we react negatively to these situations because we were so very excited that a change—potty training, sleeping in her own bed—had occurred, and the child was moving toward more independence. We look at those new actions that seem like those of a much younger child and wonder what we've done wrong.

We then decide to add a little pressure to the situation to get things moving forward again: "You know where the potty is, honey." "You're a big girl now. You can sleep in your bed by yourself."

When we can recognize how we are feeling (perhaps angry or frustrated by this unexpected turn of events) and realize that our children are probably having a developmentally normal regression, we can accept where our children are in the moment. When we meet them there, in that gap between where we think they should be and where they actually are, we are actually able to help them move forward more quickly than if we fight a situation that is normal. During these times, there is generally brain reorganization going on, and our children need us in the old way, the way they did before the big step forward, for just a little while longer. If you can accept that this is where your child is, everything will move along better.

Emotionally regulate yourself and put yourself in your child's shoes. If you are able to do what she is asking of you, such as lay beside her in her bed until she falls asleep, do it. But do it with a willing spirit or don't do it at all. It is better to set a limit if you are unable to do something for your child joyfully, and take responsibility for how you feel, than to do something you don't want to do and blame your child.

We all do the best we can at any given moment. It is true. If your child is unable to buckle himself into his car seat one day, he is still doing the best he can. Children want to please their parents. When we look at times when our children don't please us as a situation where they *can't* do what we say, rather than that they *won't* do as we say, there is a very different outcome. We have a little more patience with our child, which creates connection.

Think about your parenting experiences, especially those times where things didn't go as you had hoped they would go—you know, the times where you ended up yelling at your children or throwing something down on the floor in frustration. Ask yourself, were you doing the best you could at those times? You probably were. If someone told you to try harder or act your age in those moments, would it have helped you to do better? Probably not. Those are the times where you needed someone to connect with you, to understand why this situation was so difficult for you, to empathize with your circumstances so that you could move through your frustration, your anger, your sadness, or your fears.

I can hear you saying, "But my child's behavior is unacceptable. I cannot accept this behavior right now! Are you crazy? I can't let him think it is all right to act this way."

This is true: we all need to learn what is acceptable behavior and what is unacceptable behavior. Accepting where your child is and that he is doing the best he can in the moment is only part of the process. Later, when you're both regulated, is the time to talk about your child's behavior and other ways of handling those situations where good choices are not being made.

Turning Conflict into Connection

So what does our tendency to regress into lower brain states when stressed have to do with nurturing relationships? Quite a bit, actually.

If you look at your child and you are generally smiling when you think of her, situations where you lose it may be few and far between. You're probably mostly staying out of negative feedback loops with your child. Even when you do have a hard day, you may be able to apologize to your child fairly easily and find the good in her. Your brain states probably stay within the range of the prefrontal cortex, or rational, thinking brain, only sometimes moving into the emotional brain. And your child will be more likely to stay in her rational, thinking brain too.

Remember that nurturing relationships is about taking those situations when there is a conflict and finding a way to make it a positive connection. What would it even look like to focus on the relationship in the bedtime situation described at the beginning of the chapter?

Let's start again: It is bedtime, and you're tired. You tell your child to go to bed, and he rolls his eyes at you. Oh boy! This is the part where you stop and breathe. It is your job to stop the negative feedback loop because you are the parent. Adding in the pause before acting will help by giving you at least a moment to stop yourself, before you do something you'll regret. If we want our child to be able to pause when he experiences a conflict and not simply react, we need to model this pause, so that he'll know what it looks like and feels like.

I admit that most parents have difficulty at first learning to add the pause. One father described his experience: "Our son was heading for a meltdown again over not wanting to brush his

teeth. I was apparently out of patience and found myself exploding at him. As it was happening, I saw an image of a red stoplight
and had a fleeting thought go through my head about losing 50
IQ points, and I knew that now would be a good time to stop.
But I just couldn't stop right then, even though I knew I wasn't
going to make the best choices. Of course, it was a disaster. It
took over an hour after that to get our son calmed down and into
bed. I apologized for being unable to make the best choice and
for the words that I had said to him. He seemed to understand
and gave me a big hug."

This father continued to work on his own emotional regulation at those times that were particularly upsetting to him.
Eventually he found himself able to pause and then become
emotionally present and connect to his son's emotional state.
Even though you may not remember to pause or be able to
pause at first, keep working on it. You'll get it!

Sometimes when parents can see a trouble spot for
themselves in their parenting, but continue to react in the same
way, there is often a little more going on that needs to be ad-
dressed. When one of our own unmet needs from childhood is
being triggered in a situation with our own child, we need our
own tools and someone other than our child to help us move
through it. One of the best tools for the job is Hedy Schleifer's
Crossing the Bridge. This wonderful tool allows your partner to
support you (or vice versa) and create a safe environment as you
dig down deeper into whatever is stuck and bring it up to be seen
and acknowledged. When this emotional clearing is completed,
you won't feel the same charge when the situation comes up with
your child. If you don't have a partner, Crossing the Bridge can
be used with a close friend or family member who is willing to
simply reflect back what you're saying. Dealing with your own
unmet childhood needs in connection with another adult goes
a long way in clearing the space between you and your child,
so you can be more emotionally present.

Back to the bedtime request. After the eye roll, you pause and realize that your son must be having a hard time. You move in a little closer to have a conversation.

You (in a calm voice): You just rolled your eyes. What's that about?

Your child: You're always bossing me around! I'm in the middle of a game and that doesn't seem to matter to you.

You (reflecting back what your child just said): It feels like what is important to you doesn't matter to me.

Your child: That's right!

You: I'm sorry you feel that way. I see that you're playing a game right now. When would you be willing to stop playing for the night and go to bed?

Your child: How about after I finish this game I'm playing right now?

You: How long will that take?

Your child: About another ten minutes or so. Would that be OK?

You: That sounds good to me.

If you pause, take few deep breaths, and choose to not react to the negativity your child displayed, the situation can have a very different outcome. Instead of yet another power struggle, you would be able to understand that the eye roll really wasn't about you; it was about your child not feeling like his needs were important. Once you're able to hear your child, both of you can get your needs met. You can meet your need to be heard and to see your child get the rest he needs. Your child will also feel heard and know that what he wants is important to you. Most importantly, the situation can end with connection rather than disconnection.

Nurturing Through Transitions: The Illusion of Not Enough Time

It seems that everyone is in a really big hurry. We have schedules to adhere to, bosses who insist we're at work at a particular time, minimum household tasks that must be done to keep the health department or family services out of our homes, activities for our children, all of which leave us feeling frazzled and always in a hurry. We don't have time for dawdling!

We forget about this present moment, the one right now. Just stop for a moment and breathe it in before you read any further. Look around you. What do you see? What do you hear? What do you smell? What is touching your body? How do you feel? Are you hungry? Tired? Sad? Excited?

Our children live in *this* moment, the one right *now,* all the time. And yes, it is our job to be the adult and to actually plan ahead, but we can do that and still respect this present moment and our child's need to be in it. It can actually be a wonderful lesson for us as parents to remember to make time to just be here now.

When we're out of this present moment, we may find ourselves reacting from the past or fearing for the future. Perhaps our situation brings up messages from our childhood about the importance of being on time to events or our commitments. These kinds of messages can get in the way of us seeing our child who is immersed in the bubbles from washing her hands. When our parenting decisions are made from a place of fear for the future, we're also out of the present moment. If we find ourselves thinking that if we don't teach our child the life skills necessary to get out of the house in the morning in a timely manner, then he is "never going to learn," we're in a place of fear. We will be unable to see the playful ways we might be able to encourage our child through the process of getting ready, and we will create disconnection, rather than connection.

When we feel there isn't enough time, we hurry our children. And when we hurry our children, they feel our stress and begin to express their stress in ways that actually slow everyone down. Have you ever experienced this scenario when you're in a hurry to get out the door? As you notice the clock ticking closer to the time you need to be at your destination, you begin to feel more and more stress. As your own stress level goes up, you notice your toddler or preschooler, or even an older child, slowing down. They still haven't eaten. Shoes are still lost. Your stress level goes up another notch. You're now firmly in the orange-light territory (the one between a yellow-light state and a red-light state—I suspect you've experienced what I'm talking about), and it isn't looking good. This is probably the moment when your preschooler spills her orange juice all over herself and needs a change of clothing, shifting you fully into a red-light state. It isn't pretty.

The more rushed you are, the more unlikely it is that you'll be able to access creative solutions to your challenges and get everyone out the door feeling good and connected to each other. Consider planning lots of time and limiting your commitments when your children are not making transitions, such as leaving the house, easily. Building in more time will create more opportunities to add in play, because you won't be feeling rushed or overwhelmed.

New Behavior? What's Changed?

When a new behavior pops up for your child, always ask yourself, "What has recently changed?" I often ask parents that question and hear stories about how they just lost their home and had to move in with Mom's parents, or they just had a new baby, or someone just died. It isn't a coincidence that children's behavior changes when there are big changes in the family or with family members. Even if you aren't telling your children what happened, they still feel that something is wrong, and they assume it is about them.

Consciously Nurturing Relationships at Different Ages and Stages

Now that we have an idea of what the essential pieces of relationship-focused parenting look like in practice, let's see how we can nurture relationships with our children during various stages of our parenting journey, from the time our children are infants until after they become adults. As a bonus, we'll also see how grandparents can apply relationship-centered techniques when caring for their grandchildren. For each of the following scenarios, I've given the traditional, behavior-focused advice for handling the situation, followed by relationship-centered guidance. See which resonates with your experience and your own inner guidance.

The Beginning of the Parenting Journey: Nurturing in the First Three Years

Ideally, parents will spent much of their children's first three years proactively creating healthy relationships, and there are many nurturing things that parents can do.

Parents of very young children often project their own fears onto their children. Our children are mirrors for difficulties we've had or developmental milestones we have not worked our way through yet.

Situation 1: Sarah and her husband, Steve, have just had their first baby, Suzie, who is just six weeks old. They have been hearing that they need to let their baby cry, or she will never learn to sleep on her own, but it doesn't feel right to leave her in her crib alone.

Behavior-Focused Advice: Babies will never learn to sleep on their own if you don't let them cry. Just put the baby down in the crib and leave. Eventually, the baby will stop crying and go to sleep. This way, the baby will learn that crib time is sleep time. She will also learn to put herself to sleep and won't need you to help her every time she wakes up. Babies who go to sleep one way will want the same help when they wake up. Teach them young, and you'll have a baby who needs you less.

Relationship-Centered Guidance: Babies are relational beings, and they communicate their distress through crying. When a mother and baby are connected, it is nearly impossible for her to leave the baby crying. A parent who can leave a baby to cry is disconnected from the baby. Babies who are left alone do not learn to sleep on their own, though that is what appears to happen. Babies who are left alone learn that no one is coming when they are distressed. Their whole physiology changes. The cortical system in the brain becomes more sensitive to stress, which results in babies and children who are more easily upset and more difficult to soothe, as well as unable to calm their stress through relationship, as we are designed to do.

Some children become shut down or hypoaroused, perhaps appearing depressed, while others become hyperaroused and difficult to handle. There are long-term consequences for letting babies "cry it out."

Being responsive to the baby's cues is the best course of action. When the baby knows that his needs are going to be responded to, he can use his survival energies for growing and learning, rather than self-preservation.

Our infants are small for such a short time. They naturally move toward wholeness. It is our job to nurture them, to support them, so that they can unfold naturally. Children need to be respected and supported, not rushed into growing up. Take the time to hold your children as much as they will let you until they don't need to be held so often anymore. Just as a child learns to walk with the proper encouragement and opportunity, so do our children wean, sleep in their own beds, and go off to school when they are ready without our own fears getting in the way and creating more disconnection.

The choice that Suzie's parents make in this situation can lead to more connection or to disconnection. The parents can become more connected or disconnected to their own internal guidance system and to Suzie, and Suzie can become more or less connected to herself.

Sarah and Steve had a long heart-to-heart about their fears and concerns. A friend gave them Dr. James McKenna's book *Sleeping with Your Baby: A Parent's Guide to Cosleeping*, which they read together. In the end, they decided to bring Suzie into their room to sleep on a separate surface attached to their bed. Suzie was within arm's reach at night, and both parents could easily meet her needs for food and comfort. Sarah and Steve knew that one day she wouldn't wake at night and need their assistance. They understood that it was important for very young babies to wake at night and to sleep in close proximity to caregivers, as it lowers the risk of SIDS (sudden infant death syndrome). They felt comfortable knowing that they were creating good nighttime connections with their daughter in a way that worked for their family.

Note: If you feel that your child is in great distress or you are overwhelmed in parenting and waiting for your child to move out of a particular developmental phase, it is important to address these concerns. See Book II of the Consciously Parenting Series, *Creating Connection,* for a more in-depth discussion about early behaviors and how our stories are a big part of these kinds of conflicts, as well as how to move through them in a way that is respectful to everyone.

Situation 2: Jill had been breastfeeding her son, Harry, age two, but had been feeling a great deal of resentment toward him for constantly needing to be near her. Jill wanted to wean, but didn't want it to be traumatic for Harry.

Behavior-Focused Advice: Go on a trip without the baby, or put hot sauce on your nipple so that it is a negative experience for him to nurse. No child needs to nurse for two years, so he just needs to get over it. If you're done breastfeeding as a mom, it is over. Give him a pacifier and a sippy cup. He'll be fine.

Relationship-Centered Guidance: Breastfeeding was about so much more than the milk for Harry. This had been part of his life since the day he was born. Nursing had helped him to calm down during times of stress and created a special closeness with Mom that nothing else could match. It was important for Jill to acknowledge just how important breastfeeding is to Harry, regardless of the outcome.

Jill was having very strong feelings about her son needing her. Where was this coming from? What happened when Jill was a child and needed her mother? Was her mother able to meet Jill's emotional need for her presence, or did her mother push her away? Before Jill could make an informed decision about the best way to proceed, she needed to look at her own needs and understand them better.

It wasn't healthy for Jill to continue to breastfeed and feel resentful toward Harry. Harry undoubtedly felt this resentment and began to believe that his needs were bad; eventually he would think that *he* was bad for wanting to be close. This was a recipe for relationship disaster, with future repair work written all over it! So Jill needed to make a choice: wean Harry or work through her own feelings about breastfeeding and having someone close to her who needed her. If she chose to wean, she needed to understand that she would be losing a parenting tool and that Harry was still going to need her, perhaps in a different and somewhat more intense way than before. Children's needs, when met, will go away. A need unmet is here to stay. (See guiding principle 3 of Consciously Parenting.) Harry's need for closeness would still need to be met, whether she continued to breastfeed or not. That's why Jill needed to work through her negative feelings about his need to be close, no matter what choice she made regarding breastfeeding.

When children feel that we are pushing them away, they tend to move in closer and cling more. This was what was happening with Jill and Harry. The more Jill resisted Harry's attempts to move in closer, the more Harry demanded that he be allowed to be right on top of her. It was a big negative feedback loop.

After spending some time looking at her own history, Jill decided that it was important for her own sanity that she wean. She was anxious to do this in a way that maintained connection in the relationship. She decided that she would wean Harry gradually, instead of cold turkey, and that weaning wouldn't involve any trips away from her son. She would respect his need to be close to her and give him lots of physical and emotional connection time with her to make up for the closeness of the breastfeeding. She started by eliminating one nursing after he woke up from his nap in the afternoon. During this time, they ate a snack together and went out for a walk. If Harry was very distressed, she would allow him to nurse.

Jill reduced his nursing down to just once or twice a day and found that this was something she could live with for the time being. Within a few months, he had given up nursing on his own. Jill felt proud of herself for meeting the needs of her son and for still respecting her own feelings.

Consciously Nurturing Relationships with Children Ages Three to Five

Children this age are moving into more independence, but are still very young. They need a great deal of attention and guidance to become healthy and happy adults. They still need lots of help with emotional regulation, especially if what happened to them in their first three years did not support a healthy, connected relationship with their parents. Children who were left to cry it out or who experienced birth trauma or other early life traumas, such as adoption, are more likely to need additional assistance at this stage of development than children who had most of their early needs met by emotionally present adults.

This is the age of learning to balance the young child's needs for independence and for dependence. It is always respectful to ask if they would like help or not. Sometimes they need gentle encouragement to try to do something on their own, but don't force them.

Situation: Shannon contacted me because her five-year-old daughter, Melinda, was refusing to go to kindergarten. Shannon wanted to do the right thing, but she was confused about how best to handle this situation.

Behavior-Focused Advice: Children need to learn how to separate from their parents. Have the teacher hold the child while the parent leaves. After enough experiences like that, the child will learn that she has no choice in the matter and will go into school without a problem.

Relationship-Centered Guidance: Melinda was communicating that she was overwhelmed at the prospect of going to school. Learning more about what was going on with Melinda when she was calm and regulated would help Shannon make the best decision for her.

It is never OK for a child to be left somewhere against her will, with no say in the matter or with no one acknowledging her feelings. Ignoring a child's needs and feelings creates a disconnection in the relationship.

School is a long-term commitment, and it is always better for children to have a positive association with school in the very beginning rather than a negative one. Children are ready for transitions at different times, depending upon their own early experiences, and everyone will be ready for such big changes at different times. It is OK if the child isn't ready for kindergarten at five and parents choose to delay the start of school for a while.

I suggested that Shannon give Melinda lots of extra time in the morning before school to prepare for the transition. During this time, Shannon was to give Melinda more attention—holding Melinda on her lap or spending some quiet time together, with Shannon being fully present—to prepare for the separation. (Shannon would be "filling up Melinda's love cup" in parenting expert Pam Leo's words.) I also suggested that Shannon talk with the school to see what the staff, starting with Melinda's teacher, were willing to do to make drop-off time easier for everyone. I suggested that Shannon spend a lot of time talking to her daughter about school when Melinda was relaxed, perhaps in the evening around bedtime, and work to understand exactly what her fears were. She and Melinda could also practice the transition by pretending that Shannon was dropping Melinda off and picking her up again.

Shannon decided to try the nurturing suggestions and work with the school for a few weeks and then, after that time, re-evaluate how Melinda felt and decide if she was ready for school or if Shannon wanted to just keep her home. Shannon had several meetings with the kindergarten teacher and school administration members to determine the best course of action for her daughter, creating a support team on site to ease Melinda's transition into school. Shannon was allowed to go into the classroom in the morning and sit quietly in the back until Melinda had settled and was ready to let Shannon go home. Even though Shannon worked part time, she had the flexibility in her schedule to allow for this, and it was a real blessing. Having Shannon stay in the classroom for a little while helped Melinda to start to feel more comfortable, and Shannon began to see that she was doing well in the new environment.

If Shannon hadn't had the job flexibility or if the teacher or school officials weren't open to working with her, Shannon would have had to decide whether it was specifically this school environment that was not working for Melinda or whether it was school in general. If it was the particular school, I would have suggested that she do some more research to determine the best placement for her daughter. Were there schools nearby that may be a better fit?

Shannon also worked with the school to find a "safe person" for Melinda within the school— a teacher, a staff member, or even a volunteer with whom Melinda could connect during the school day and who would also watch out for Melinda's needs and commit to a relationship with her beyond academics. They developed a relationship with the school social worker, who agreed to help Melinda transition into the classroom. Melinda was also allowed to request a visit with the social worker if she became overwhelmed during the day. She actually never had to do so, but she felt better and safer because she knew that she could.

After several weeks of Shannon taking Melinda into the classroom every day, Melinda asked to walk in by herself: "I'm OK now, Mom. You don't need to come in with me today." As the school year continued, there were days when Melinda was less happy about going, but she was able to work out her feelings mostly by herself.

If Melinda hadn't been able to handle this transition, Shannon would have been happy to keep her home from school for another year to allow her to unfold a bit more on her own, knowing that it was a matter of time before she was ready. Just as children eventually learn to walk with little help when they're ready, children handle other major transitions best when their own pace is respected.

Consciously Nurturing Relationships with Children Ages Five to Nine

Between the ages of five and nine, children are really expanding their worlds. This is often the time that children go to school full time and have other adults who are a big part of their day. It is also a time when peers become a much more dominant part of their lives. We need to understand that our children need us to be present when we are with them, and they need us to support them as they navigate relationships outside of the family, by listening to them, intervening in the new relationships when necessary, and limiting our children's choices when necessary. Children of this age need parents to be parents, to keep them safe and to be an advocate, while teaching them how to proactively navigate challenges in their world. For most families, this is often the time children go to school full time and have other adults who are a big part of their day. Regardless of school setting, it is also a time when peers become a much more dominant part of their lives.

Situation: Seth was diagnosed with allergies, including a very severe peanut allergy. It was very important that this seven-year-old learn what foods were safe for him to eat and that he learn to make food choices independently. It was a tremendous responsibility for a young child to handle, but it needed to happen. His parents, Donna and Dave, were unsure how to handle this situation in a way that was respectful.

Behavior-Focused Advice: Tell the child what will happen to him if he eats peanuts and remind him daily about the consequences of his actions until he is too scared to eat anything unless given to him by his parent. He can learn later about the foods that are safe for him to eat.

Relationship-Centered Guidance: Donna and Dave needed to put themselves in Seth's shoes. How difficult must it have been to have so many restrictions on the foods he was allowed to eat? For parents, many feelings will arise about this kind of situation, including the parents' own fears about what could happen if the child accidentally ate the offending food. Donna and Dave needed to work through those feelings before making any decisions about Seth and how to proceed.

When we connect with the feelings of another, we are more likely to make decisions that respect that person. And we are modeling for our children how to respect other people.

Once Donna had come to terms with the situation and figured out which foods were acceptable for her son to eat, she sat down with him and explained what was going to change and what he needed to know. She told him that eventually he would be able to make those decisions for himself, but for now she would be guiding his decisions to make sure he understood what he could eat. She used the concept of stoplight eating from William Sears's book *Eat Healthy, Feel Great!* and let him know which foods were green-light foods, yellow-light foods, and red-light foods for him. Green-light foods could be eaten as much as he wanted. Yellow-light foods were foods that he could eat on occasion, and red-light foods were foods that were simply not allowed on his diet because they would make him ill.

Donna also listened to Seth's feelings about the foods he would be unable to eat—those foods that used to be his favorites but were now on the red-light list. Together, they came up with alternatives they could try and recipes they could make together to replace some of those favorites he was missing. Donna turned the situation into an opportunity to connect more with Seth.

After a short time, he was able to make his own decisions about the foods that were available to him, and Donna worked with him to always make sure there were appropriate alternatives that were acceptable to him and helped him to stay on the diet that would keep him healthy. Seth learned how to keep himself safe, and he and his mom had a much better relationship.

Consciously Nurturing Relationships with Children Ages Ten to Twelve

Children of this age will ask for more freedom. It is still your job as the parent to set safe boundaries and help them avoid situations where they may be overwhelmed. Remember, they are still young and need you to help make decisions for them, even if they don't act like they need you.

Situation: Travis wanted a cell phone. Even though he was only ten, he claimed that all of his friends had cell phones and that he was the *only* kid without one. His parents weren't very excited about the idea of Travis having a cell phone at all.

Behavior-Focused Advice: Tell him that he is not allowed to have a cell phone—end of discussion. Or just get him the cell phone and don't worry about it.

Relationship-Centered Guidance: Travis's parents called a meeting to discuss this issue. Dad started by asking Travis why he wanted a cell phone and what he would do with it. His parents listened to Travis share that he really felt left out of his peer group because he didn't have a cell phone. When Travis felt heard, his mom asked if he would be willing to listen to their concerns about him having a cell phone. He agreed, so they shared about their concerns about the cost and about the exposure of his growing brain to the electromagnetic field (EMF) emitted by a cell phone.

Dad suggested that maybe a pay-as-you-go phone would work for Travis because he didn't need many minutes. Travis could buy a phone and a certain number of minutes. This way,

Travis would have a cell phone if he really needed it, but he wouldn't have the expense of a monthly cell phone plan. The pay-as-you-go phone plans are self-limiting, so Travis wouldn't be able to use more than his paid-for minutes. Everyone agreed that the expense of the minutes would be Travis's responsibility, making the cell phone a safe opportunity for him to learn about money, as well as how to use the phone's technology. Everyone also agreed that they would prefer Travis had a phone with a speaker option, and Travis promised to use the speaker feature whenever possible.

A month later, Travis had had his new phone for several weeks, but really had barely used it. He had felt heard by his parents, and a connection had been created through the positive resolution of this issue. Even if his parents had said that he couldn't have a cell phone, he knew that his parents cared about his wishes and that there was always space for a discussion. How many ten-year-olds have that experience?

Consciously Nurturing Relationships with Teens

Listen, listen, listen. And listen some more. Validate feelings. Set boundaries (see the previous section on ten- to twelve-year-olds). When teens feel they can trust you, they will come to you for encouragement and suggestions when they are having a problem. If they don't trust you, they will turn to their friends. Create safety in the relationship, so teens can come home and connect with someone who loves them even when they make mistakes.

If something is too overwhelming for them, you'll know it because of their behaviors. For example, if they aren't ready to use a cell phone responsibly, they will likely use more than the allotted minutes. If that happens, gently set a boundary when you are both calm (e.g., "I can see that it is too overwhelming for you to use the cell phone because you went over your minutes by 500 last month. What do you think we need to do about that?") Encourage problem-solving and work with them to come up with solutions to challenges, rather than coming in and telling them what to do.

Situation: Sabrina agreed to do the dinner dishes: loading them into the dishwasher, starting the dishwasher, and emptying it when it was finished running. Dad walked into the kitchen to find the dishes still sitting in the sink and Sabrina on her computer on Facebook.

Behavior-Focused Advice: The parent needs to take charge and turn off the computer. If she doesn't go in and do the dishes right away, she can forget about her computer for the week!

Relationship-Centered Guidance: Dad took a nice deep breath and went in to talk to Sabrina.

"I notice that you're on Facebook right now," he said. "Did you remember about the agreement we had regarding the dishes?"

Sabrina shrugged her shoulders and continued typing.

"This is important, honey," Dad went on. "This isn't like you to disregard a task that you said you would do. What's going on with you?"

"I just don't feel like doing it right now," Sabrina replied.

"We depend on your help with some of those tasks, and you're usually really good about doing them without being reminded. I'm wondering if you're not feeling well."

"Yeah, my stomach hurts a little bit, so I wanted to just sit and rest while I played on Facebook for a few minutes. It is starting to feel better now, so I'll get up in just a few more minutes and go take care of the dishes. Sorry that I didn't tell you what was going on with me in the first place."

"That's OK. Thanks for letting me know now."

The dishes got done, and the relationship stayed intact. Dad knew his daughter enough to know that shirking her responsibility wasn't like her. The relationship they had allowed him to give her the benefit of the doubt. And he was able to avoid escalating the situation by remaining calm himself.

Consciously Nurturing Relationships with Adult Children

Parenting doesn't end just because your child has turned eighteen, no matter some people would have you believe. You are always someone's parent no matter how much you'd like to think that your responsibilities are done. There will always be worry or concern for the wellbeing of your child and for the choices that she will make in the world.

Nurturing connection while launching adult children means that we respect the needs and concerns of our child, yet we also expect that they will respect our needs and feelings as well. It is a time of transitioning into an adult-to-adult relationship, rather than a parent-to-child one. Take the time to discover what is going on with your young adult and to understand what fears and concerns he has regarding the changes that will be happening in the coming months and years.

If the young adult will be attending college away from home, there is a definite date when things will be changing. If college is not part of the plans or if your child will be attending college from home, this is time to negotiate some new ground rules. For example, talk together and decide together what expenses need to be shared and what each person will be responsible for. Provide opportunities to talk about budgeting, expenses, and where money will be coming from. Address your own fears and whatever concerns you may have about your child's ability to handle life on his own.

Young adults still need to have connection with their parents. The human brain doesn't finish developing until we are approximately twenty-five years old! Figure out what you can do to create connection with your young adult now. It is never too late.

Situation: Rayanne and Donald were anticipating their son's graduation from high school in a few weeks. Jeff had been homeschooled his entire school experience, with the exception of a few apprentice experiences with some local artists during the past year. He was a gifted painter, and his parents wanted him to have the experience of working with those who could guide him forward.

Jeff had not had many experiences outside the home. Rayanne and Donald had limited his exposure to the computer and to TV. He had spent time only with his church youth group and a small, local homeschooling group. Donald in particular was concerned that Jeff wasn't ready to handle life on his own because he had been sheltered from the outside world. I shared my concern that Jeff might really express his freedom in a negative way when he went off to college. We brainstormed about ways to meet Jeff's needs for autonomy and prepare him for the experience of college while he was still at home.

Behavior-Focused Advice: Make him get a job when he goes to college and have him pay for his expenses in college. He'll learn how to handle his responsibilities, and he'll be too busy to get into much trouble. Everyone goes to college and makes bad choices.

Relationship-Centered Guidance: Rayanne and Donald agreed to a conversation with Jeff, admitting their concerns. They asked Jeff what it had been like to have limits put on him. Jeff responded that he didn't like it very much. Through the conversation, they decided that Jeff would be able to have access to the computer and that he needed to figure out a way to monitor his time. He was able to handle this task, so they decided to give Jeff a bit more freedom.

Jeff decided to get a part-time job so that he could start earning his own money on a regular basis. Rayanne helped him to develop a budget for the monthly expenses that he would have when he went to college, and they scheduled biweekly meetings to discuss how he was doing.

Now Jeff is a college sophomore and is doing well, living about ninety minutes away from his parents. They still have a close relationship and look forward to his monthly visits home.

Consciously Nurturing Children with Special Needs

Recently I was struck by a Facebook post written by a mother of two children with autism. She was being hard on herself because she couldn't be the peaceful parent she wanted to be. My heart went out to her. I can only begin to imagine her struggle, knowing how difficult it has been in my own life with two children who don't have special needs. Many of the families I work with do have children with special needs of all kinds, so parenting children with special needs comes up a lot.

Extra time for everything is a good rule of thumb for nurturing relationships when there are special needs. This means extra time for transitions, but it also means extra time for parental self-care. One child under the age of six needs four emotionally mature adult caregivers, according to research shared by Dr. Bruce Perry, a neuroscientist and psychiatrist out of Texas. For children with special needs, the ratio needs to be much higher, so that no one person is doing all the care for a child. However, I often find that parents feel they can't let someone else care for their child, so they are very undersupported.

We can't nurture someone else when we are depleted. The best thing you can do to nurture your child with special needs is to make sure that you have enough support and that your own needs are being met.

Relationship-Centered Grandparenting

Being a grandparent seems like the best of both worlds from where I am right now, deep in the trenches of parenting. As a grandparent, you get to enjoy the children, to play with them, to connect with them, but you don't have the responsibility of the day-to-day parenting. Grandparents have such an important role to play in both the lives of their own adult children and the lives of their grandchildren. It takes a village to raise a child, and children need many special people in their lives who believe the sun rises and sets around them. Parents today have many, many demands on them in addition to raising the children, and most of all parents need support. We all need to feel special, and grandparents can be such an important part of that experience for their grandchildren, as well as their adult children.

Consciously Nurturing Relationships with Your Adult Children Who Are Now Parents Themselves

It seems to be difficult for many grandparents to accept that their children are grown and now have responsibilities of their own. It must be difficult to move beyond the role of parent and create a relationship of equals, but it is one of the most important things you can do for your adult children. Reading this book and understanding the choices your daughter or son is making regarding parenting is a big step in the right direction. Two of my clients are a mother and daughter, and together they have been taking all of the classes available through my website. They study the information together and help each other to practice and apply the ideas in their own lives. Grandma lives nearby and comes over on a regular basis to be with the children. This is a tremendous help to her daughter, not only to have the relief of someone helping with the children, but also because her mother understands and practices relationship-focused parenting.

Create a friendship with your adult child and learn to listen to her. If you didn't have a connected relationship in the past with your adult child, now is the time to create one. If you made mistakes as a parent, apologize for them. Even if you weren't a model parent while your child was growing up, you can start being the example of the kind of parent you want your own child to be for her children.

Learn as much as you can about child development and the needs of children. Information is very different than it was when you were raising your children, so make the investment in your grandchildren and learn all you can.

Respect your adult child's parenting choices. If you disagree with him on something, consider having a conversation with the intention of understanding why he is making the choice he is making. Arguing will not make a difference, but listening may. If you can see that some of your own parenting choices have made an impact on your adult child's ability to meet the needs of your grandchildren, let him know it and apologize. Remember, you were doing the best you could do with the information you had available to you at the time.

Consciously Nurturing Relationships with Grandchildren

Love for grandchildren is often spelled *time.* Plan to invest time with your grandchildren and let them know that you are making a special effort to connect with them. If you are a long-distance grandparent, plan to call at least once a week and talk on the phone.

You may need to work to develop your own style as a grandparent. What kind of grandparent do you want to be? What do you want your grandchildren to always remember about their time with you? What do you remember fondly from your time with your own grandparents? What do you choose to create with your grandchildren? The sky is the limit. Just make sure that you take the time and let your grandchildren know just how incredibly special they are. It can be the most important thing that you ever do.

Questions to Ponder

- What are your current stressors?

- What are your child's current stressors?

- Are there any previously unresolved experiences of shock or trauma you discovered from the previous chapters? Write them down. This will give you an idea of your current stress load. What can you do to create a little more compassion for yourself and your own story?

- What is one situation where you'd like to turn conflict into connection? Write down what normally happens and then write down how you'd like it to go. Choose an action step.

Conclusion

Nurturing relationships with your children and with your partner is a daily practice. Unless we happened to have been blessed with parents who nurtured each other and nurtured us, even when we may not have "deserved it," we may not know quite how to create this kind of loving connection with our children. With awareness, we can create healing through our day-to-day experiences for ourselves and for our families.

Every day, many times a day, we choose connection or disconnection in our families. Nurturing relationships is about recognizing when our loved ones are in an emotional place, whether we understand what is happening in their world or not, and making the space to connect. We often think that if we respond to our children when they are emotional that we will be reinforcing their bad behavior. In reality, we all need to learn to connect when we're in an emotional place. Learning different behavior happens later, when we are no longer in our emotional brain. The deepest healing happens in relationships where there is vulnerability and connection at emotional times. This is especially true of our relationships with our children.

Nurturing connection cannot happen without an awareness of your own needs. We cannot nurture someone else when we are depleted.

We looked at different ways we can all nurture relationships in our daily lives, including physical touch, emotional presence, simplicity, rhythm & rituals, community, and play. We explored ways we all get stuck when trying to nurture our relationships with our children by looking at the story that we all bring into parenting from our own early life experiences. We also looked at our children's stories and how they affect our relationships with them. Handling feelings (your own and your child's) and creating room for connection when they're happening was explored in Chapter 3, as well as understanding the role of shock and trauma in one's story. We discovered ways of communicating verbally and nonverbally in which we are nurturing the ones we love. Finally, we explored how we can nurture our relationships with our loved ones as we make parenting decisions at different ages and stages.

In my next book, Healing Connection, we'll be taking a much more in-depth look at what it really takes to repair relationships between parents and children, between partners, and heal family relationships where there has been much disconnection in the past. We'll also be exploring healing trauma, including adoption, birth trauma, and other losses that happen in our families. Book IV is the final book in the Consciously Parenting series and it will be available in 2014.

Appendix 1

Comparing Behavior-Focused and Relationship-Centered Parenting

Behavior-Focused Parenting	Relationship-Centered Parenting
Focus on chronological age "Old enough to know better" or "Too old for that!"	Focus on emotional age and making observations
Rules, authority, and control most important	Relationship and loving influence most important
Ignore or invalidate feelings	Acknowledge and validate feelings
One-sided conversation	Conscious communication
No boundaries or rigid boundaries	Boundaries
Parent is always right	Apology

Appendix 2

The Guiding Principles of Consciously Parenting

Principle 1: All behavior is a communication. Behavior reflects the internal state of the individual and the relationship's level of connection.

Principle 2: The parent-child relationship is more important than any behavioral intervention, consequence, or punishment.

Principle 3: Children unfold neurosequentially, and quality, connected relationships allow for the unfolding. A need met will go away; a need unmet is here to stay.

Principle 4: Behaviors occur on a continuum. Behaviors in children (and parents, too) correlate to the parents' own neurodevelopment and attachment status.

Principle 5: Parental interpretation of behaviors comes from both a conscious and subconscious place, resulting in positive or negative neurophysiologic feedback loops.

Principle 6: All individuals have a right and a responsibility to learn to express their feelings appropriately. Feelings allow us to connect to our internal guidance system.

Principle 7: Children need boundaries. We can set appropriate limits for our children while still respecting their needs and feelings—if we are aware of ourselves. (We can ask, for example, "Is this about me? Is this about them? Are my children communicating a need? Is the boundary I'm setting necessary, or is this situation an opportunity for me to grow?")

Principle 8: No man is an island. We need to create communities of support for ourselves and for our children. We need to take care of ourselves so that we can take care of our children.

Resources

Books

Affect Dysregulation and Disorders of the Self by Allan N. Schore

Attached at the Heart: 8 Proven Parenting Principles for Raising Connected and Compassionate Children by Barbara Nicholson and Lysa Parker

Becoming Attached: First Relationships and How They Shape Our Capacity to Love by Robert Karen

Biology of Belief by Bruce Lipton

The Boy Who Was Raised as a Dog by Bruce Perry

Connection Parenting: Parenting through Connection instead of Coercion, Through Love instead of Fear by Pam Leo, website: www.connectionparenting.com

The Continuum Concept by Jean Liedloff

The Family Bed by Tine Thevenin

Healing Trauma: Attachment, Mind, Body, and Brain, Edited by Marion F. Solomon and Daniel J. Siegel

The Healing Power of Emotion: Affective Neuroscience, Development, and Clinical Practice, Edited by Diana Fosha, Daniel J. Siegel, and Marion F. Solomon

The Hidden Messages in Water by Masaru Emoto

Hold Me Tight: Seven Conversations for a Lifetime of Love by Dr. Sue Johnson, website: www.iceeft.com

How to Talk So Kids Will Listen & Listen So Kids Will Talk by Adele Faber and Elaine Mazlish

Immaculate Deception II: Myth, Magic, and Birth by Suzanne Arms, website: www.birthingthefuture.org

Keeping the Love You Find: A Personal Guide by Harville Hendrix

Let the Baby Drive: Navigating the Road of New Motherhood by Lu Hanessian, websites: www.letthebabydrive.com, and www.parent2parentu.com

The Making and Breaking of Affectional Bonds by John Bowlby

Molecules of Emotion: Why You Feel the Way You Feel by Candace B. Pert, PhD

The Neurobiology of "We": How Relationships, the Mind, and the Brain Interact to Shape Who We Are by Daniel Seigel (audio book)

Nonviolent Communication: A Language of Life by Marshall Rosenberg

Opening Up: The Healing Power of Expressing Emotions by James Pennebaker

Parenting From the Inside Out: How a Deeper Self-Understanding Can Help You Raise Children Who Thrive by Daniel J. Siegel and Mary Hartzell

Parenting From Your Heart: Sharing the Gifts of Compassion, Connection and Choice by Inbal Kashtan

Playing in the Unified Field: Raising and Becoming Conscious, Creative Human Beings by Carla Hannaford

Raising Our Children, Raising Ourselves: Transforming parent-child relationships from reaction and struggle to freedom, power and joy by Naomi Aldort

Real Love by Greg Baer

The Science of Parenting: How today's brain research can help you raise happy, emotionally balanced children by Margot Sunderland

Siblings Without Rivalry: How to Help Your Children Live Together So You Can Live Too by Adele Faber and Elaine Mazlish

Sleeping with Your Baby: A Parent's Guide to Cosleeping by James McKenna

Three in a Bed: The Benefits of Sleeping With Your Baby by Deborah Jackson

Trauma Through a Child's Eyes: Awakening the Ordinary Miracle of Healing by Peter A Levine and Maggie Kline

Waking the Tiger: Healing Trauma by Peter Levine

Why Love Matters: How Affection Shapes a Baby's Brain by Sue Gerhardt

The Womanly Art of Breastfeeding published by La Leche League, website: www.llli.org

Writing Down Your Soul: How to Activate and Listen to the Extraordinary Voice Within by Janet Conner, website www.writingdownyoursoul.com

<u>You Can Heal Your Life</u> by Louise Hay

Additional Resources

Attachment Parenting International, website
www.attachmentparenting.org

Bay NVC, website www.baynvc.org

Carrie Contey, website www.slowfamilyliving.com

http://www.elephantjournal.com/2012/04/skip-your-morning-
meditation-watch-this-instead/

Center for Nonviolent Communication, website www.cnvc.org

Connection Parenting, website: www.connectionparenting.com

Hedy Schleifer, LMHC, website: www.hedyyumi.com

Holistic Moms Network, website www.holisticmoms.org

Infant Massage USA, website www.infantmassageusa.org

International Chiropractic Pediatric Association, website:
icpa4kids.com

Interview with Janet Conner:
www.consciouslyparenting.com/teleseminars/JanetConner1.php

Kindred Community, website www.kindredcommunity.com

La Leche League International, website www.llli.org

Mindsight Institute, Dr. Daniel Siegel, website
www.mindsightinstitute.com

Mothering Magazine, website www.mothering.com

Parent2ParentU, website www.parent2parentu.com

Pathways to Family Wellness Magazine, website
www.pathwaystofamilywellness.org

Ray Castellino and Mary Jackson, *Little People, Big Challenges*.
www.consciouslyparenting.com/LPBC
Website: www.aboutconnections.com

William Sears, MD. Website: www.askdrsears.com

Reactive Attachment Disorder Resources:

Dr. Daniel Amen, Amen Clinics: http://www.amenclinics.net

Eric Guy, Center for Victory: www.centerforvictory.com

Dr. Bruce Perry, The Boy Who Was Raised as a Dog,
www.childtrauma.org

Karyn Purvis: http://empoweredtoconnect.org

Shock and Trauma Resources:

Masgutova Method: http://masgutovamethod.com

Jin Shin Jyutsu: http://jsjinc.net

Jin Shin Tara: http://www.tara-approach.org

BEBA (Building and Enhancing Bonding and Attachment): http://beba.org/

Rebecca Thompson is also trained in shock and trauma, and she offers individual consultations. You can email her directly: Rebecca@consciouslyparenting.com

For additional resources and recommended practitioners, please visit:

www.consciouslyparenting.com/resources